BEATING THE SYSTEM

The True Story of a Horse Racing Legend

Copyright © 2017 by Jerry Bader

All rights reserved. No part of this book may be used or reproduced or transmitted in any form or by any means, electronic of mechanical, including photocopying, recording, or by an information storage system, without permission from the publisher.

Published by MRPwebmedia
www.amazon.com/-/e/B06XNLBWT1

BEATING THE SYSTEM

The True Story of a Horse Racing Legend

by Jerry Bader
Author of "The Fixer"

Illustrated by Paola Ceccantoni

Preface

This is my life. My name and the names of the people and places have been changed for obvious reasons, but the incidents and experiences described all happened. This is real life, not a phony Hollywood version that demands things be packaged in a neat familiar framework with no loose ends. My life is full of loose ends, and many of them are still walking around.

To understand my story you have to understand the underlying principles that formed my personality, and guided me through a dangerous underground existence that reeked of corruption, greed, and danger. As a Jew whose parents survived the Nazi concentration camps I learned life is fragile, and survival arbitrary. As a jockey I developed an approach to life of living in the moment, of pushing the envelope, of reacting first, because not reacting can cost you the race, or maybe your life.

Jockeys are modern day serfs that travel the country picking up rides where possible, for the most part earning scraps, guaranteed to be seriously injured. Did I bend the rules? Yes. Did I break many of them; most certainly, because that's the way the game is played. Horse racing is a microcosm of society where the rich get richer, and the rest of us do what needs to be done to survive. Don't fall for that nonsense that everybody can be President or Prime Minister, that anybody can be the next Steve Jobs or Warren Buffet. To be blunt, that's horseshit.

I did what I had to do to survive, and I make no apologies for it. I knew wise guys, even my best friend was one, but I was wise enough to know, that's a dead end, especially for an outsider. And I knew I would always be an outsider, a Jew, a jockey, and a fixer. So this is my story, it's not a journey wrapped in a nice neat package, it's life as it really is, raw, crude, and dangerous. This is my life; it's how I lived it; I hope you enjoy it, and maybe even get a few laughs out of it.

Enjoy,
Alias Ronny Kleinberg

Table of Contents

Prologue

Be Careful Who You Screw

Part I:

The Formative Years

Deaf and Dead

The Camps: Just Don't Stumble

Don't Mess With The Little Heb

Cabbage Town

Part II:

The Jockeys

A Close Call – The Machine

Welcome To The Sport of Kings

The Game Is Don't Get Caught

Payback's A Bitch

The Double Double-Cross

Thank You Black Beauties

The Mudder

Seeing Red

Different Strokes For Different Folks
A Middle American Pit Bull
The Wrong Place At The Wrong Time
Some People You Shouldn't Fool With
Dually Noted
The Almost Union

Part III:
The Gamblers, Gangsters and Crackpots
Killer Chickens
One Crazy White Boy
Two Cops, A Gangster, And A Hawaiian
A Shot In The Ass
The Cuban
What Twenty Thousand Buys
It's Not Always Skeletons In The Closet
Not Quite Routine
Bobby The Bug Man
Take Your Medicine Like A Man
You Win Some And You Lose Some

Part IV:

The Veterinarians, Trainers and Agents

Daryl, The Horse Doctor

Daryl's Damaged Horse Power

Disorder In The Court

Like A Bee Is To Honey

Oh Brother!

Daryl Versus Tesio

Who Owns The Moral High Ground?

Not All FBI Agents Are Mormons

Mission Accomplished

Get Out Of Town And Don't Come Back

Running A Ringer

Punch Drunk Agent

Rich, Cheap, And Stupid

I'm No Rat

Part V:

The Women

And So It Starts

Annie Get Your Son

Unlucky In Love

Crazy Bitches Part One

Crazy Bitch Part Two

You Gotta Know The Password

You Don't Have To Be Married To Be Screwed

Eventually You Learn Your Lesson

The Contest

Part VI:
More Than Just Horses

Doctor Death and The Picture

The Kentucky Standoff

Smooth Operator

Bonus Material

Ten Things You Need To Know To Win At The Racetrack

Ten More Things You Need To Know To Win At The Racetrack

Life is messy

Prologue

Life is messy. It's neither a journey nor a path, instead people plod, meander, or lurch from one defining incident to another. The fact that our lives are superficially remembered with glib Kodak moments only hides the ugly truth. Life is chaotic, and no one's life was more chaotic than Ronny Kleinberg's. It would be unfair to try and cram Ronny's wide-ranging experiences into a nice neat package with a clear-cut beginning, middle, and end. And so I start in the middle, because that's as good a place to start as any.

Be Careful Who You Screw

Joey Pines kneels on the bathroom floor of the Juanita Bar on the outskirts of Detroit. Pee is trickling down Pines' soiled jeans pooling on the floor around his knees. Blood runs down his face from where Ronny introduced his nose to the Mexican's Smith and Wesson. The guy is scared, scared to death, scared because in the next few seconds a decision had to be made. Does Joey Pines end his days on the bathroom floor of Juanita's third-rate bar, or does he live another day so he can screw somebody else? Whatever happens, he's never going to screw Ronny again.

It all started three days earlier when Ronny fixed the fifth race at Motor City Downs. Fellow jockey, Angel Morales, came to him with a deal. Juan Carlos Perez, a local drug dealer wanted to expand his operation. He was already supplying jockeys with various illegal pharmaceuticals for weight loss and entertainment purposes, so why not expand into the gambling business. Perez supplied the money, and Morales supplied Ronny. It was an arrangement made in hell.

The fifth race at Motor City Downs seemed like the perfect initial foray for Perez. All the jockeys in the race were paid their five hundred bucks and given the order of finish for the first three horses. Other than the first three places, jockeys could do what they wanted but those first three horses had to finish in the correct order for Morales, Perez, and Ronny to collect on the trifecta. This wasn't rocket science.

Everyone was on board but Ronny had his doubts about Pines, who was a known shithead and drug addict. Someone had seen Pines slip the valet what looked like cash, probably for a bet. If Pines was betting on the race, was he betting the trifecta, or was he betting on himself? Nobody knew for sure. Before the race Ronny warns him.

"You understand what you have to do? Your number can't be on the board. You fuck us over and finish in the top three... you'll be in the ground before the sun comes up."

"Don't worry, I got it."

As the horses were being loaded into the starting gate Ronny turns to Pines one more time. "We good?"

Pines nods, "I got this."

The starter rings the bell and the gates fly open. Coming around the first turn Ronny is on the outside of Pines, they're in sixth and seventh places respectively. Ronny looks over at Pines and sees him pull up his sleeve. The prick has a machine. Before Ronny can do anything about it he hears the buzz, and Pine's horse takes off leaving Ronny and everyone else in the dust. They get to the finish line and Pines finishes second. The horses that needed to finish one, two, three, finish first, third, and fourth. The bet is busted. The son-of-a-bitch screws Ronny and friends. He doesn't even collect on his own bet because he came in second instead of first. Pines is laughing and making fun of the other jockeys who all had bets on the race, figuring it was a sure thing.

Morales approaches Ronny, "My friend… what are we going to do? Carlos will be pissed, he's out a lot of money because of that little prick."

"Call Perez and tell him to wait for my call." Morales leaves to call Perez while Ronny continues changing into his street clothes, all the while keeping an eye on Pines as he continues ribbing the jockeys who lost money. Ronny waits for Pines to leave and follows him out into the parking lot. Ronny gets into his car and watches. Pines gets into his car; he reaches across to the passenger side and opens the glove box. He takes out a small plastic prescription bottle and dumps a small amount of powder onto the back of his hand. He takes a rolled-up bill from his pocket and shoves it up his nose snorting what is obviously cocaine. He starts his car and leaves. Ronny follows.

They drive for about fifteen minutes until Pines pulls off the road into the parking lot of Juanita's Bar, a third rate dive on the outskirts of town with cheap drinks and hookers to match. Ronny pulls in and parks on the opposite side of the parking lot. He waits in his car for about fifteen minutes allowing enough time for Pines to get a snoot full. Ronny enters Juanita's and spots Pines at the bar drinking, laughing, and having a jolly old time. Ronny goes directly to the payphone and calls Morales.

"Angel… you with Perez… Good… He's at Juanita's. Get over here fast. I'll keep an eye on him." Ronny finds a seat in the corner and orders a beer while waiting for the Mexicans. About ten minutes later they show up and spot Ronny sitting in the corner. They join him at his table.

Ronny looks at Perez and asks, "Did you bring your piece?" The Mexican nods affirmative. "We're going to take this little prick out.

You just follow my lead." The three men sit and wait. After about five minutes Pines gets up to go to the bathroom. Ronny and the Mexicans get up to follow.

"Perfect," says Ronny. "Angel you watch the door and make sure nobody comes in. Perez and I will take care of this *cabrón*." Ronny and Perez follow Pines into the bathroom while Angel guards the door. As Pines gets ready to use the urinal Ronny grabs him by the shoulder with his left hand spinning him around, while his right hand crosses over connecting squarely on Pines' jaw. Pines goes down. He's on his knees shaking. Ronny slaps him hard across the face. Pines begins to cry, pee is running down his leg pooling under his knees.

"You're not laughing now, are you, asshole? Look at this prick... crying like a baby." Ronny slaps him hard again. He looks over at Perez who's standing to his right slightly behind him holding his Smith and Wesson Model 39 Automatic. "Shoot the asshole!" But Morales just stands there transfixed.

"Please don't shoot, I've got a wife and kids..."

"You should have thought of that before you screwed us. I saw you plug-in your horse. You think I don't know a machine when I see one?"

"Please... I'll make it up to you... please don't kill me... please!"

Ronny slaps Pines again just to shut him up. He looks at Perez who's standing there with the gun pointed at Pines, seemingly paralyzed.

"Jesus Christ... are you going to shoot this asshole or not?" Perez opens his mouth but no sound comes out. "What a chicken-shit. Give me the fucking gun!" Ronny grabs the gun out of Perez's hand. He shoves the gun in Pines' face, "Say your prayers asshole, and say'em fast!"

Pines is blubbering something about mercy and he'll never do it again or some such shit, but it's mostly incoherent. Between the tears, the pee, and the snot running down from his nose into his mouth nobody could understand what he was saying. Ronny is disgusted. He takes the gun and in a big sweeping motion smashes Pines across the head. Blood starts pouring from Pines broken nose. He's a mess but alive. Ronny takes the gun and slaps it into Perez's chest.

"Some fucking gangster you turned out to be. Don't call me again. We're done." Ronny walks out of Juanita's bathroom, through the bar and out to his car.

"Those who cannot remember the past are condemned to repeat it." - George Santayana

Part I

The Formative Years

Deaf and Dead

During the Second World War Ronny's Grandfather on his mother's side was blowing up German ammunition dumps. He gathered his wife and children together and told them that it was only a matter of time before the Germans would catch up to him. He knew he was living on borrowed time but he had no intention of going to the camps; he would not be taken alive.

Eventually the Germans tracked him to his brother's home where he was hiding. His brother was deaf. A small, group of soldiers arrived at his brother's house. When they asked his brother where Ronny's Grandfather was he didn't reply because he couldn't hear them. When he didn't answer the Sergeant's question immediately, the Sergeant pulled out his Luger and shot Ronny's Great Uncle in the head. Ronny's Grandfather was hiding in the bedroom. When he heard the shot he ran out of the bedroom firing his gun killing the Sergeant and the next three soldiers that tried to enter the house. Eventually reinforcements arrived and Ronny's Grandfather was killed.

The Camps
Just Don't Stumble

You don't have to be a concentration camp survivor to feel the effects of one of history's most heinous chapters, but if you're the son or daughter of someone who was in the camps you can bet the odds are you too will be greatly impacted. Ronny's father survived the camps because he had a skill that the camp Commandant found useful. He was a bootmaker, and the only thing Nazi officers liked better than their perfectly tailored uniforms, was their perfectly fitting boots. They'd strut around like male peacocks exhibiting their feathers for the opposite sex. But useful or not, one wrong move and your body would be found in the mud or sent to the gas chambers.

Even if you survived, your existence was horrifying. Surrounded by death, disease, depravity, and starvation, made for desperate people willing to take a chance, even if it ended in a bullet. Some even welcomed it, a quick end preferable to a slow painful demise. The camp rules were unbending, break them and you'd be dead in an instant. If you stole anything, they'd shoot you; if you stumbled and fell, they'd shoot you.

In the morning the prisoners would line up in a row to go to their assigned jobs. Ronny's father was weak from diarrhea and stumbled. He felt a hand grab him from the back so he didn't fall. If you fell, the guard would point to the fallen prisoner and then to the tower. The guard in the tower would put a bullet in the unfortunate prisoner's head. That day could have been his father's last. He turned to thank whoever saved him, but there was no one there. He was the last one in line. Someone or something grabbed him from behind stopping him from falling, saving his life.

These are the stories Ronny grew up hearing. These are the life lessons that shaped Ronny's personality. They reminded Ronny of his father's philosophy of life: everyone has an alarm clock shoved up their ass, and when it goes off, your time is up. On that day in the camp, someone, or something, decided that his alarm clock should stay silent. It's a philosophy of living in the moment, for the moment, a philosophy that almost caused Ronny to put a bullet in Joey Pines' head.

A jockey's life was supposed to save Ronny from a life of crime.

Learn more in "The Fixer" - Rebel Seed Publishing

Don't Mess With The Little Heb

You can watch documentaries of the Nazi concentration camps and feel a profound sadness at man's inhumanity to his fellow man, but listening to your own father tell you stories of his personal experience in the camps is life altering. That kind of experience will ultimately color your world view and your approach to living in what was a hostile land. Today Toronto is one of the most cosmopolitan, ethnically diverse cities in the world, but it wasn't always the case. Even those of us whose families managed to escape the direct trauma of Nazi Germany remember the stories of Toronto's ethnic rumbles. The infamous riot at Christie Pits and the signs on the sand in the Beaches area that defiantly announced "No Dogs or Jews Allowed."

It was these influences that affected Ronny's approach to life. When you're surrounded by hatred and violence you have two choices, you become a victim or a villain. At five foot nothing, barely registering a hundred pounds Ronny was smaller than almost all his high school classmates. You would think that being so small he'd be the first on the list of any potential bully to harass, but in the words of Ira Gershwin, "It ain't necessarily so."

Every school has its bully and Ronny's downtown institution was no exception. One particular punk was a large kid with a following of future Don Jail inmates. The punk and his posse would prowl the school picking fights and causing trouble with a special emphasis on the Jewish kids. If anyone complained, the uptight pinched cheeked churchgoers that operated the educational asylum would resort to a feeble "boys will be boys" refrain. The one person these teenage hoodlums didn't bother was Ronny. Even as a kid, despite his diminutive stature, he exuded a 'don't fuck with me attitude.' Like most bullies they knew when to let sleeping dogs lie, but sometimes, ethnic contempt can get the best of a punk who should know better.

Ronny and his friends were playing pool one Saturday afternoon at a local pool hall that tolerated under-aged kids. The place was dingy and dark with two pool tables that had long since seen their prime. The place emitted an aroma of body odor and bad breath but Ronny and his friends didn't care. It was a cheap afternoon's entertainment that for the most part kept Ronny and his buddies out of trouble. On this particular afternoon the school thug showed up. Ronny's friends were playing a game of snooker while Ronny waited off to the side for his turn. As soon as the bully spotted Ronny's friend's he launched into a series of ethnic slurs and taunts. When that didn't get a rise out of Ronny's friends he proceeded to get physical, grabbing their pool cues, and making threatening gestures while continuing his verbal onslaught of cultural anti social diarrhea.

The elderly owner of the establishment suddenly decided that there was something of great importance he had to do in the backroom. At that point Ronny stepped forward and whistled, one very loud, piercing whistle. The bully turned to see Ronny holding a pool cue in the manner one might expect from a samurai warrior. The punk smiled a sheepish smile and moved for the door with Ronny following.

The bully headed for his bike but Ronny closed fast with the pool cue still in his hand. When Ronny got close enough he swung the cue around connecting with the back of the punk's legs knocking him to the ground. Ronny drops the cue and grabs the kid's bike. As the kid starts to get up Ronny hits him hard with the bike, the pedal landing squarely on the kid's nose. Blood starts gushing from the bully's nose and the beginnings of some very prominent welts start to form on his hard empty head. All the kid can do is fight back with feeble threats of retaliation.

"Wait till Monday at school."

"Why wait, we can settle this right now."

"I'll see you Monday."

"I'll be waiting."

Monday rolls around and Ronny and his pals are just hanging around talking when the shamed school tough guy and his gang of miscreants walk by. The kid has a big white bandage across his broken nose, a doozy of a shiner, and several well-placed lumps on his head. One small kid standing behind the bully decides today is the day he's going to get brave. So he steps out in front of the bully and challenges Ronny, figuring the head hard-ass will have his back. As Ronny takes a step towards the kid, the bully grabs his pal and pulls him back in line. He looks at Ronny almost admiringly and says.

"Don't mess with that little Heb, he's crazy. You'll only get hurt."

When your parents tell you stories of what they went through in the camps, you become determined to never let it happen again. Every challenge needs to be confronted. Every bully needs to be put down. And every situation demands survival.

Cabbage Town

Ronny wasn't doing well in high school so he transferred from an academic school to a technical school, Central Tech. Ronny's new school drew a lot of students from Cabbage Town. The area got its name from the poor immigrant inhabitants who planted cabbages on their front lawns in order to have something to eat.

Today, Cabbage Town is a gentrified area of Toronto, home to many diverse creative and professional people, but back in the day it was a rough part of town populated by Irish, Polish, and Macedonian immigrants all trying to eke out a living. Most of whom had little affinity for the Jews who found themselves in their midst. The infamous riots of Christy Pits between the Jews and Italians of the Harbord Playground Baseball Club and the Swastika flag waving supporters of the Catholic Church sponsored Bathurst and Bloor Club were a thing of the past, but neither community had forgotten. Nor had the Jews forgotten the signs on the sand in the Beaches part of town that read, "No Jews or Dogs Allowed." Ronny found himself at Central Tech High School with these lingering remnants of distrust and a residue of hatred left by the riots of Christy Pits and the indignity of the Beaches' insults.

Ronny was a five foot, ninety pound Jew in a school controlled by the Jackson Gang, led by Mickey Jackson, a six foot, two hundred pound, blond, blue-eyed specimen that would have looked right at home in a Hitler Youth uniform. His three perpetual companions were equally large and equally Aryan in attitude. These gangsters in training watched the weekend wrestling matches on television starring the likes of Sweet Daddy Siki, Edouard Carpentier, and Whipper Billy Watson. They would come to school on Monday morning with vivid images of elbow smashes and drop kicks. They'd practice their newly learned moves on anyone that dared get in their way. Mickey Jackson thought it would be a safe bet to try one of his elbow smacks on the diminutive future jockey when his back was turned, but Ronny felt him coming. He wheeled around catching Jackson in the jaw with a single right hook.

As Ronny stood over the felled attacker, he warned him. "Start with me you oversized piece of shit, and you won't like the outcome."

Later that day in gym class, Jackson, surrounded by his familiar bully brotherhood, started picking on Ronny. They started by throwing basketballs at him in warm-up, and during the game they used every opportunity to elbow, punch, and abuse Ronny. The gym instructor found no problem with teaching the little Jew a lesson. After the game when the teacher left for his office, two of the Jackson boys grabbed Ronny and held him down while another watched the door. Mickey Jackson then beat the crap out of Ronny. When they finished, Ronny was bruised and bleeding. The four senior members of the Jackson gang stood over Ronny smirking and laughing.

Ronny got to his feet and gave them a second warning, "I warned you the first time and you didn't listen, and now I'm giving you a second and final warning. Go home and don't come back to school this afternoon."

"Is that right? The little Jew is giving us a warning, a final warning no less," says Mickey. His three buddies all respond with laughter. As they turn to go, Mickey adds one more final taunt, "Maybe you should think twice before coming back yourself. This was just the preliminary round."

Ronny wipes the blood from the edge of his mouth, "You want to play hardball, asshole, then that's exactly what we're going to do."

The Jackson Gang leaves the gym laughing and joking at their revenge. Ronny went directly home. On one side of Ronny's house lived a concentration camp survivor that knew Ronny's father from the bad old days; the other side was home to a couple of young collectors for a real crew of wise guys. Mort was a Jew, while the other was black; everyone called him Midnight. Ronny was friends with these two real gangsters. They told Ronny if he ever ran into any trouble at school to just let them know and they'd take care of it. When Ronny got home for lunch, he went directly to Mort and Midnight's place.

Mort looks at Ronny's face. "What the hell happened to you?"

"The Jacksons' thought they could start up with me."

Midnight shakes his head. "We'll take care of this. After school you point these pricks out to us and we'll do the rest."

Throughout Ronny's life he always seemed to have backup. When he was a kid it was Mort and Midnight, and when he got older it was Salvatore Latorre, the mob enforcer.

They waited until school was about to get out. They then piled into Midnight's 1956 T-Bird and headed for Central Tech. Mort, Midnight, and Ronny leaned up against the car watching as the kids came out of the school for the day.

Mort touches Ronny's shoulder, "You point out the four guys who did this, then get on a bus and go home. You don't want to be here when this goes down."

Ronny spots the four members of the Jackson Gang still laughing and joking about their big victory, "That's them there, that's the four pricks that beat me up." But instead of going directly home as instructed Ronny walks across the schoolyard right up to Mickey Jackson. "I warned you not to show your face after lunch."

Ronny points at Mickey, then turns to Mort and Midnight who are approaching quickly, "This one is the leader…" Ronny turns back, "Now you're going to learn how a real beating is done." Then Ronny walks away. The entire school is watching as Mort and Midnight take apart the Jackson Gang. When all was said and done the four members of the gang lay bruised and broken on the ground in front of the entire school. Mickey Jackson was bleeding badly from his right eye where Mort caught him with a left hook; one of the others lay on the ground moaning from the broken rib inflicted by one of Midnight's expert karate kicks to the midsection. When they were done Mort and Midnight got into the 1956 T-Bird and went for a drink. The four Jackson Gang members were picked up in ambulances and taken to Toronto General Hospital.

By the time Ronny got home a yellow police squad car and an unmarked police car were parked in front of his house. When he walked in two Detectives were waiting for him in the parlor. Ronny went into the kitchen where his father was waiting, He asks Ronny what happened. Ronny tells him the story. His father doesn't say a word; he just brushes a finger across his lips, signaling Ronny to keep his mouth shut.

Ronny sits down across from one of the Detectives. The other is standing off to the side. The sitting Detective tells Ronny, "You're going away for five years. Mickey Jackson almost lost an eye."

"I guess that prick picked on someone his own size this time."

"Did you do it?"

"Me! I weigh ninety pounds for God's sake."

"Look, we already know who did it. All you have to do is tell us, and we'll leave you alone."

"Fuck off!"

The Detective's not used to people talking to him that way, let alone a kid, a smartass Jew no less. "What did you say?"

"What? Do I stutter or something? These pricks gave me a beating this morning. I wasn't there when they got beat up."

"Then you're going to jail."

Ronny sticks his hands out waiting for the Detective to handcuff him. "Here, go ahead."

Now the other cop speaks up, "So what do you think happened?"

"These guys are bullies. They're always picking on people trying to show how tough they are. Like I said before, they must have picked on the wrong guy and they got what they deserved."

The standing Detective signals his partner that they're leaving. "We're going to keep our eyes on you, so I suggest you keep out of trouble."

On the way out, one of the Detectives notices the 1956 T-Bird parked in the driveway next door. He elbows his partner to take a look, "Nice car!" And they leave.

The following Monday Ronny goes back to school. When the Jackson boys finally get out of the hospital and come to class, they keep to themselves and don't bother anybody anymore. One of the Italian kids comes up to Ronny in the schoolyard.

"Hay... Kleinberg, wait up."

Ronny stops and waits for the kid, "Yeah what's up?"

"Thanks, we all appreciate you looking after the Jacksons."

"Me? I had nothing to do with it. They just picked on the wrong guy,"

"Sure," the Italian kid says, "the wrong guy for sure."

Sometimes you beat the system,
and sometimes the system beats you.

Part II

The Jockeys

A Close Call – The Machine

The more you learn about horse racing the more you realize cheating is an integral part of the sport. It's not like Ronny and a few other outliers were the only ones that did it. Many of the riders did it, and not just the low level jockeys traveling the bullring circuit. Big name jockeys, in big-time stake races did it. And it's not like everybody didn't know; starters, stewards, trainers, horse owners and even track owners knew what was going on. And don't think it doesn't happen today, because it does.

Cheating in horse racing is like prostitution; you can't stop it, so occasionally the authorities try to control it. Since 1974 the authorities have documented three hundred incidents of machine use. In the 2000s alone there have been fifty-three cases, and that's just the times jockeys have been caught.

A machine is a small electrical device consisting of a Triple-A battery connected to a couple of prongs. Jockeys usually hide them under a wristband, under the sleeve of their silks, at least that was Ronny's favorite place to hide it. It allowed for easy access when he wanted to plug-in a horse, as well as making it readily available to dispose of on the track after it was used, or if he was under suspicion of having one on his person. You use the machine by zapping the horse on a nerve in its neck. If the horse is what's called a 'machine horse' it will shift into high gear and hopefully win the race. Not every horse responds to a machine, so a jockey or trainer has to know if a particular horse will react to being plugged-in.

Ronny had several close calls involving carrying a machine. While riding in Montreal, Ronny was suspected of using a machine. The authorities have to catch the jockey with the gizmo on them in order to make an accusation stick. Ronny had developed a number of strategies for getting rid of a machine before they could find it on him, but this time the starter was determined to catch him.

The head starter stands on a platform overlooking the starting gate while assistant starters help load the horses into their positions. Once the rear gates close the head starter usually starts the race in a few seconds, but if he suspects somebody of carrying a machine he's got them trapped. On this occasion Ronny was sitting in the sixth hole. There were ten horses in the race. All the horses were loaded and Ronny hears the rear gate open. Two assistant starters begin dragging his horse out of the gate.

"What the hell are you doing?" complains Ronny.

"You're carrying a machine. Get off your horse and take off your silks."

Ronny refuses, "No, you can't do that."

"What do you mean, I can't do that?"

"Read the rule book," Ronny says, "you can't just take me out and nobody else, it's prejudicial. You have to unload everybody and check each rider in order by gate number. Read the rules."

It's total bullshit of course, but Ronny figured the starter didn't know the rules any better than he did, so they start unloading all the other horses giving Ronny time to think of something. Now all the assistant starters were busy unloading the other horses and only one starter was holding Ronny's horse. Ronny takes his feet out of the irons seemingly turning control of the horse over to the assistant starter.

The assistant starter is pushing the horse in one direction and Ronny is pulling it in the other. In the confusion Ronny sees a gap and turns his horse around facing the wrong direction. He hits the horse with the machine and it takes off knocking down the assistant starter. The horse and Ronny charge down the backstretch in the wrong direction giving Ronny the opportunity to drop the machine that disappears into the track dirt. Now that Ronny's gotten rid of the machine he turns the horse around and heads back to the starting gate.

The head starter looks down at Ronny and asks, "What the hell do you think you're doing?"

"All this confusion got the horse upset. I didn't do anything."

"Get off the horse and take off your silks," demands the head starter. Now Ronny doesn't care. He complies and removes his silks in the middle of the backstretch. Of course they don't find a machine. The head starter notices the wristband Ronny is wearing so he asks.

"Why are you wearing a wristband?"

"Why do you think," says Ronny, "I have a sore wrist."

"Get back on your horse, you smart ass son-of-a-bitch!"

Ronny gets back up and wins the race without using the machine.

There are many strategies for getting rid of a machine.
Learn more in "The Fixer" - Rebel Seed Publishing

Welcome To The Sport of Kings

Sometimes the catching of machine riders becomes more of a game than a serious attempt to stamp out the practice. There was a head starter down in Florida that took a different approach to solving the problem. Ronny was entered into a race with nine other horses. The starter, a good guy that got along with everybody, and who knew the score, got everybody in the starting gate, and then looking directly at Ronny made an announcement.

"I'm taking a lot of heat from the brass because you chaps are using machines." The head starter is still looking directly at Ronny. "So when I open the gate, I want to see a bunch of gizmos lying on the ground, so I can take them back to show the stewards, so they know I'm doing my job." The gates open and the horses take off. Five machines, including Ronny's, are lying on the ground.

Later that day the head starter comes into the jockey's room and sees Ronny, so Ronny asks. "Why were you looking at me?"

The head starter says, "Because I know you had one."

Nothing was done. The stewards and the starter showed they were on the lookout and everyone was happy. Business continued as usual with horses getting plugged-in and races getting fixed. Welcome to the sport of kings.

The Game Is Don't Get Caught

Ronny was in Detroit riding for a Kentucky hardboot hillbilly by the name of Chester Thurman. The fellow had a large farm with thirty horses and Ronny was his jockey. Thurman's best horse, Brick House, had won a couple of low level races but nothing special. When Ronny started riding him he realized the horse was a machine horse. For the horse to be a consistent winner, it would have to be plugged-in.

Plugging-in a horse involves zapping it under the neck with a small device that gives the horse a minor electrical jolt that causes it to take off and run faster. It doesn't work with all horses but with certain horses it's just the incentive they need to get to the finish line first. Plugging-in a horse is illegal and if you get caught with a machine you can get suspended for a year. The trick is not to get caught.

Once Ronny started to plug-in Brick House, it started to win consistently. One day Thurman comes to Ronny and asks in a soft-spoken slow shit-eating drawl, "Mister Ronny... somebody told me you've been electrocuting my horses."

Ronny could hardly keep a straight face. He had to bite his lip not to laugh, "Chester," he said, "I would never do such a thing to your fine horses."

"All right then," Thurman says, "I just thought I should ask." Meanwhile Ronny keeps plugging-in Brick House and he keeps winning. Thurman decides that Brick House is ready to move up to a Starter Series. It's a series of races that start off at one mile and gradually increase to two miles. As the races get longer the purse increases until the final two-mile race is worth ten thousand dollars plus a bonus. Ronny and Brick House do well in the series and win three out of the four preliminary races leading up to the big finale. Ronny's horse is the favorite in the final payoff race.

Ronny reads in the racing form that someone is bringing in a horse from Chicago and when Ronny looks at the horse's record he knows he can't win. The horse is just that much better than Brick House and all the other horses entered into the race. The track is a Bull Ring, meaning it's a short track. In order to run a two-mile race, the horses have to go around the track three times. Bull Rings have tight corners and short straight-aways and they put a premium on a jockey's ability to handle the track. If you're too fast into the turns you can cause an accident but if you don't go fast enough down the straight-aways you won't win. A Bull Ring race is the equivalent of short-track Olympic skating, anything can happen, and it usually does.

Race day comes and Ronny notices the owner and trainer of the Chicago horse have so many tickets on their horse they need an elastic band to keep them together. They're betting on the fact they've got a sure thing. The race goes off and Ronny takes the lead; two times around the track and Ronny and Brick House are still in the lead. As they head for home the Chicago horse makes its move. As it gets up to Ronny the jockey whips the horse into its final stretch drive. As the Chicago horse passes Ronny he brushes by Brick House. Ronny knows he's done, so he grabs Brick House's mane and stands up as if the Chicago horse hit him hard enough to knock him off stride. The Chicago horse wins by five lengths.

As the jockeys pull-up down the backstretch Ronny rides up to the Chicago horse and asks the jockey, "Hay jock... you got something for me?"

The other jockey laughs, "Fuck you! You got to be kidding me. I beat you by five lengths."

Ronny repeats his request, "I'm going to ask you one more time. You got something for me?"

The other jockey just smirks: "Get lost," and he rides off.

When they get back to the winner's circle Ronny notices that both the Chicago horse and Brick House's numbers are flashing on the board, meaning there's a Steward's Inquiry into the bumping incident. After the jockeys do their post race weigh-in a call comes in from the Steward's office. Normally the Stewards ask each jockey what happened and then make a decision. This time the phone rings and they ask for Ronny only. He picks up the phone and the Steward says, "He bothered you didn't he?"

Ronny answers, "Yes Sir he did."

"Good enough," says the Steward.

Five seconds later the Chicago horse's number comes off the board and Brick House wins the race. The owner of the Chicago horse is mad, and he approaches Ronny with a fist full of tickets. Evidently he had a thousand dollars bet on the horse that went off at 6:1. It would have paid six thousand dollars if it hadn't been disqualified. Ronny looks the owner in the eye and says, " You should have got a different jock. He's stupid."

The owner doesn't understand, "Why?" he says.

"I asked him twice if he had something for me, and twice he told me to get lost. If that's the way you play the game, this is what happens. Next time get a smarter jockey."

Payback's A Bitch

Ronny was good friends with a fellow jockey Gary Southgate. While in Montreal Southgate and Ronny shared a locker. The lockers in a jockey's room aren't really lockers, because you can't lock them. They are just wooden cubicles where the jocks can stow their street clothes and gear. Ronny and Southgate shared one of these cubicles.

There is a rack in the room where all the silks for that day's racing are hung. A program for the day's races is cut up and displayed so that the valet can check which rider has which mounts on that day's racing card. The valet takes the silks for each race and hangs them in the appropriate jockey's cubicle.

The day's racing was over and Ronny had just finished his shower and was starting to get dressed. Southgate was still getting undressed to take his shower. He takes off his boots where he has two hundred dollars worth of tickets on the horse he rode in the last race. Jockeys can't bet on races that they're participating in, but it's not unusual for an owner or trainer to slip a ticket or two down a jockey's boot as an extra incentive before a race.

The horse Southgate was riding won and paid eighteen dollars making for a substantial payday for the jockey. He asks Ronny to go and see how much the tickets are worth while he takes his shower. Since it was a big payday he offers to take Ronny out for a drink. Southgate takes his shower and Ronny checks out the tickets.

He goes to the Silk rack and looks at the program and compares it to the tickets he was handed. Ronny sees that the winning horse was number five which was the same as the number on Southgate's tickets, but when he looks at the date he notices that the date on the tickets is the tenth of the month, ten days earlier than the current date. The tickets were worthless. When Southgate comes out of the shower he spots Ronny laughing his ass off.

"What's so funny?"

Ronny hands Southgate the tickets. "Go take a look at the program and compare it to your tickets."

So Southgate goes over to where the program is posted and

compares the tickets. "So what's the problem, it's number five in the eighth race."

Ronny shakes his head. "Yeah but look at the date... Tell me something. Have you ever held this guy's horses?"

Southgate looks at the date on the program and compares it to the date on the tickets. It seems the trainer knew Southgate held his horses. He waited till he drew the same gate in the same race number and slipped the old losing tickets into Southgate's boot "Son-of-a-bitch, I'll kill the bastard."

Ronny looks at his friend and says, "I guess you should have warned him you were holding his horses."

Southgate grabs his clothes and runs out to his car with Ronny in tow. They haul their asses around to the barns looking for the trainer, but they're too late. The horse, the trainer, and his trailer are gone.

Ronny gives Southgate a bemused look, "Payback's a bitch, ain't it?"

Even when you win, you can lose.

Learn more in "The Fixer" - Rebel Seed Publishing

The Double Double-Cross

While racing in Miami Ronny ran into some trouble with the IRS who were garnishing his pay checks leaving him short of cash. A friend who was doing some business for a group of serious gamblers approached him with a proposition. Ronny's friend offers him five hundred dollars to hold his horse. Ronny tells his friend his mount is a dog, but his friend says it doesn't matter. Everyone is getting paid, guaranteeing the race is in the bag. So Ronny helps distribute the cash to the other jockeys.

Since the race appears to be a sure thing and Ronny is severely short of capital, he gives his friend a hundred bucks to bet a couple of trifectas. Ronny's friend bets a thousand bucks for himself. The race is run and one of the jockeys who was paid to hold his horse lets it run, breaking the bet. Everyone's tickets are worthless. Ronny and his friend are hot. They decide the offending jockey needs to be taught a lesson.

Ronny follows this jockey into the shower. The jockey turns on the water and Ronny calls his name. He turns around and Ronny hits him square in the face. The jockey goes down and

Ronny hits him a couple more times. Ronny is standing over the guy who is sprawled out on the floor. The water from the shower pours down creating a river of red from the blood gushing from the offender's nose.

"Tell me what happened. You were paid. Why'd you do it?"

"I can't. They'll kill me"

"If you don't tell me now they won't get a chance to kill you, cause you ain't walking out of this room." And Ronny hits him hard again.

By this time all the offending jockey's courage had evaporated and he spills his guts. It turned out that the gamblers who financed the whole operation screwed everybody. Knowing that everyone in the race was getting paid the gamblers figured a lot of bets would be placed on behalf of the jockeys involved, thereby lowering the odds on the winning horse. So the night before the race, the gamblers went to the chosen jockey who was suppose to hold his horse and paid him an extra five hundred dollars to let his horse run. He was told to keep his mouth shut or they'd kill him. The double double-cross worked, netting the gamblers more than thirty thousand dollars.

Everyone has heard the expression, 'never look a gift horse in the mouth' meaning, don't question the value of a gift or in this case a fixed horse race. Evidently the expression coined by St. Jerome in the fourth century actually does relate to horses, as it was considered bad form to inspect the teeth of a horse that was given to you as a gift. But then St. Jerome never had to deal with gangsters who carried Glocks.

Fast forward thirty years, Ronny is in Florida and he runs into his old friend who got him involved in the double double-cross. He asks Ronny if he was going to the simulcast off-track betting parlor. Ronny tells him he is, so his friend says you might run into an old friend. Ronny asks who it is, but his friend says he rather it be a surprise. Ronny goes to the OTB and while standing in line he looks over and sees a not very attractive woman standing in the next line. The woman is eyeballing him. She looks familiar but for the life of him, Ronny can't figure out who she is. Then he remembers his friend telling him he might bump into someone from the old days. He looks at the woman again, and blurts out... "Holy shit... he's a woman."

The woman in the next line was the same jockey he beat the crap out of in the shower. The next time Ronny bumps into his old friend, his pal asks, "Did you recognize anybody at the OTB?"

Ronny starts laughing. "He's a woman! Can you believe that?"

"Yeah he's a woman all right... you not only beat the crap out of him, you turned him to the other side."

"I don't know about that, but I'll tell you one thing, he makes for one ugly broad!"

The Man Who Used His Own Money

Ronny has been friends with Norman Thomas since he was a young apprentice jockey. They first met when Ronny and Thomas were both in the same race. Thomas was boxed in behind Ronny but Thomas couldn't control his horse. If he couldn't get the horse under control he might clip another horse's heel causing a dangerous accident. Ronny hears Thomas yelling for help behind him so he moves to the outside creating a hole for Thomas to go through. After the race Thomas thanked Ronny and told him he owed him one. It was the beginning of a lifelong friendship.

At this time Ronny wasn't fixing races but Thomas was, but Thomas fixed races with his own money. Ronny never met another jockey that used his own money to fix races. This guy had balls... big balls. If you use your own money to fix a race you limit the number of people involved and avoid dealing with the gangsters who couldn't be trusted, and who weren't particularly understanding when things went wrong. Thomas trusted Ronny and asked him to evaluate a horse he owned. At this time a jockey would only get twenty bucks to breeze a horse, but Thomas was Ronny's friend so he did it as a favor.

Ronny takes the horse for a spin and reports back that the horse can really run, confirming what Thomas already thought. Ronny tells Thomas to keep the twenty bucks for breezing the horse and bet it for him the next time the horse runs. Instead of betting the twenty for Ronny, he bets a hundred dollars. The horse wins and Ronny picks up a big paycheck, something he desperately needed.

Thomas approaches Ronny about riding another of his horses and tells him he'll put down two hundred dollars for him to win, but Ronny says no, "If I win, I want your Cadillac."

Thomas agrees. When the race goes off, Ronny's horse takes an early five-length lead that he maintains all the way around the track until they turn for home. As they turn for home, the horse throws his head back and stops running. Ronny ends up finishing fourth losing his chance for Thomas's Cadillac. Meanwhile the five grand Thomas had down on the horse goes out the window, but Thomas is philosophical. It wasn't Ronny's fault, something went wrong with the horse. Ronny would have to get his first Cadillac some other time.

Ronny found out later that it took a year to figure out what the problem was with the horse. Horses bleed internally under the stress and exertion of a big race. What likely happened was blood was trickling down the horse's mouth making it uncomfortable causing it distress. It most likely threw back its head to swallow the blood, lost concentration, and stopped running.

The more you learn about what really goes on behind the scenes in racing the more you realize that everyone involved is a bit screwy. Years later Thomas invited Ronny over to his farm for dinner. Thomas made a lot of money out of horses and lived on a beautiful farm surrounded by a picturesque wooded lot that he owned. After dinner they started drinking, and it didn't take long for the two men to get drunk. Thomas tells Ronny that he's getting a divorce and he has to do something about the money he has stashed away.

It seems he's buried individual packets of ten thousand dollars around certain marked trees in the wooded lot around his house. He wants Ronny to help him dig it all up. Each designated tree was marked with a number that represented the number of steps from the tree that the money was buried. The trouble was, Thomas couldn't remember in what direction from the tree to dig, so Ronny and Thomas in their drunken haze spent the night digging trenches around a half a dozen trees only recovering five of the twenty-five packets of cash. Thomas wanted Ronny to come back and help him dig up the rest when they were sober, but Ronny refused saying his people weren't all that fond of digging ditches.

For every action, there's a reaction. Failure has consequences.

Learn more in "The Fixer" - Rebel Seed Publishing

Thank You Black Beauties

You don't get to be a jockey if you're not slight of build, but as you get older, maintaining your riding weight gets harder and harder. Jockeys resort to all kinds of methods to lose weight including sweatboxes, starvation, and regurgitation. Many if not all racetracks have what's called a *heaving bowl* where jockeys can purge the contents of their stomachs before being weighed. The jockeys call it *flipping*.

During Ronny's racing days another favorite form of self-abuse was a drug nicknamed Black Beauties, also known as Black Birds, or Black Bombers. We're basically talking about Speed, Amphetamine mixed with Dextroamphetamine.

While Ronny was racing in Detroit, the valet in the jockey's room had a connection to a doctor who would provide prescriptions for a price. The valet would make the rounds taking orders from the jockeys. The packages of one hundred pills would then be distributed to the jocks with payment due on payday, which was usually Friday.

This little pick-me-up not only reduced the jockey's appetite, it also created a mild euphoria, caused increased hyperactivity, and reduced the ability to sleep. Today Black Beauties have been replaced with methamphetamine. The drug was not without some unfortunate side effects like talking to yourself and obsessive grinding of teeth. Ronny was not the only jockey that ended up having to have his bottom teeth replaced with implants.

But replacing teeth was not the only consequence of the Black Beauty weight loss regime. Ronny had a horse in the third race that needed to get out of the gate fast if it had a chance to win. Ronny remembers sitting beside this jockey who was entered in the same race and who had the slot beside him in the gate. Ronny was just next to him on the inside. Ronny asks the jockey if he'll give him some room coming out of the gate. "No problem!" he says.

But the guy is making Ronny nervous. He's all fidgety and he's chewing nonstop on his teeth. This guy is high as a kite. As they get ready to enter the gate Ronny asks this jockey again if he'll give him some room. "Sure, sure, no problem!" But this guy is just too high to trust so Ronny eases out of the gate instead of going full bore. Good thing, because the juiced jockey is so ramped up he comes out of the gate like a bat out of hell pushing three horses into the rail, wiping out the whole field. Luckily no one was badly hurt.

When they got back to the jockey's room Ronny sarcastically says to the guy, "Thanks a lot for giving me some room."

To which the other jockey replies, "Yeah sure, no problem, anytime." The guy had no idea what he had done. Thank you Black Beauties.

The Mudder

Wiping out a whole field of racehorses happens more often than you'd expect, and it can happen to anyone, even Ronny. All it takes is one wrong move and everyone goes down. Ronny was riding for an owner with a horse called Jet Liner, it was a good horse but it could only run on a soft track. The horse had what's called *shelly* feet, a condition that causes a horse's hooves to crumble easily, making it difficult to shoe the horse. Racing on a dry track hurts the horse's feet so it will stop running. The horse could only race effectively on a wet or muddy track.

Jet Liner was entered in the last race of the day. It had rained all morning so the horse had a good chance to win, but unfortunately the track was drying out. To make matters worse, the only part of the track that was still soft was near the rail, but Ronny was starting in the tenth hole on the far outside.

When he got into the starting gate Ronny told the other jockeys to give him some room because he was going straight to the rail where the track was soft. They either didn't believe him or they didn't care. When the starting bell sounded Ronny took off for the rail but the other jockeys ignored his warning. Ronny wiped out the whole field. Despite finishing first by ten lengths he was disqualified and suspended for ten days. It can happen to any rider.

Seeing Red

During the winter months all the jockeys head down south making it difficult for a lot of jockeys to pick up rides. If you aren't one of the top jockeys in the country you had to find something else to do. In Ronny's case he got a job breezing horses for a big-time owner, Jack Tomlinson, who only dealt with stake horses. For three hundred dollars a week Ronny would breeze three horses each morning. It took about three hours a day and then he was free to do what he wanted.

Two of the horses Ronny exercised were stake winners but the third was a maiden, meaning he'd never won a race. When Ronny breezed the horse he could tell it had what it took to be a big money winner. He told Tomlinson that the horse was good, in fact in Ronny's opinion the horse, Mister Red, was better than the other two horses he was exercising. Tomlinson laughed at him.

"If you like the horse so much, I'll sell him to you."

Ronny was definitely interested, "How much do you want for him?"

"Ten thousand dollars."

"I've got five I can give you now and I'll get the other five from my father-in-law."

Tomlinson agrees to Ronny's proposal but when he calls his father-in-law the answer is no. Ronny tries to explain to his father-in-law, who happens to be a horse trainer, that the horse could be worth hundreds of thousands of dollars; but he hates Ronny for marrying his daughter. He wasn't going to help even if it meant losing out on a good deal for himself and his daughter. As a result the deal was dead.

Tomlinson puts one of the top jockeys in the country on Mister Red and he runs him in a race. Ronny bets two hundred dollars on the horse, one hundred to win and one hundred to show. The horse comes in last. Ronny can't figure out what happened. The horse runs great in the morning, so there's no way it should have come in last, especially with a top jockey on him.

Tomlinson runs the horse again and Ronny bets another two hundred, and again, the horse finishes up the track. Something is very wrong. There is such a thing as a Morning Glory, a horse that runs great in the morning when everything is calm and relaxed, but in the afternoon under the pressure and excitement of an actual race, it gets anxious and chokes.

But Ronny knows this horse's temperament, desire, and ability and he just can't believe that this horse is a Morning Glory. Something must be up with the jockey and his agent. Ronny figures they're holding the horse so Tomlinson will drop it down to a cheaper claiming race where they'll pay an undervalued price. They obviously weren't aware that Tomlinson didn't believe in the horse and would have been happy to sell it to them.

Ronny goes to the jockey's agent and speaks to him. "Look" he says, "I'm not accusing you of anything, but I know this horse, I've ridden this horse, and there's no way he finishes last in those two races. Now I don't expect you to reimburse me, but I do expect you to tell me when I can win my money back."

The agent looks at Ronny for a moment, mulling over in his head what he should do. Ronny doesn't wait for an answer, "Just so you know I'm the one who exercises Mister Red every morning, and if you don't co-operate, when race day comes I'll make sure, it's not in any condition to do anything let alone win a race."

The agent reaches into his pocket and pulls out a Condition Book, which is a book issued by the Racing Secretary that lists all the races as well as what kind of horses are eligible for each race. He opens the book and shuffles through the pages until he finds a specific date. He shows Ronny the page and points to a particular race on the schedule; it's a ten thousand dollar Claiming Race. Ronny nods and leaves. When race day comes Mister Red wins by five lengths and Ronny gets his money back and more. After the race, it's announced that somebody nobody ever heard of claimed Mister Red.

When Ronny gets back to the barn, he sees Tomlinson, who asks Ronny if he knows the fellow who claimed his horse. It seems that the buyer is a trainer from Canada. It sounds like an accusation. Ronny gets hot and threatens to quit.

"Why would I pull a stunt like that and have some shill claim the horse for ten thousand when you offered to sell it to me for the same price? You want to know who really claimed that horse, speak to your jockey and his agent. I've been telling you for weeks that horse is a winner but you didn't believe me. You've been played my friend, and screwed out of a goddamn good horse."

Ronny eventually calms down and Tomlinson apologizes for the accusation. Two weeks later the new owners run Mister Red again at twenty-eight-to-one in an Allowance Race where he can't get claimed. Ronny makes his usual two hundred dollar bet, and again the horse wins easy, paying forty dollars; a nice payday for Ronny but not as nice at it could have been if his father-in-law would have gone in on the deal to buy the horse.

A while later Ronny and his wife were visiting her father's farm. The whole family was sitting in the living room watching the Derby Trial on television. The Derby Trial is the warm-up for the Kentucky Derby and Mister Red is entered. Ronny doesn't say a word. The race goes off and Mister Red wins by half a length. Ronny turns to his father-in-law.

"See that horse, Mister Red, that's the horse we could have bought for ten thousand, if you would have come up with your five." Ronny doesn't say another word. The horse goes on to win several hundred thousand dollars.

A Jew, a Catholic, and a Priest; what could possibly go wrong.

Learn more in "The Fixer" - Rebel Seed Publishing

Different Strokes For Different Folks

The next odd job Ronny came across was selling siding on credit to owners of wood clad homes. Ronny and his partner would travel around the tri-state area selling siding at discounted prices, mostly to people who couldn't afford it. Sears had a standard price for the siding of five thousand dollars. That made it easy for Ronny to lowball them with a price of four thousand dollars. Since the actual cost of the materials and labor was only about eleven hundred dollars, it left a good profit for the company, Ronny, and his partner to share.

The scheme depended on Ronny being able to get the credit applications approved from the racist loan officer at the bank. This wannabe Grand Dragon of the KKK would start each application referral with the same question. "Is the applicant, the same color as you?"

If Ronny said no, the application was rejected and the job was lost despite the occasional gift basket of chocolates containing a thousand dollars cash. But Ronny had a knack with people, and when he dealt with African-American customers he would be straight and tell them the bank were a bunch of assholes that wouldn't approve the loan, but he would give them an extra discount if they paid cash. More often than not, being honest paid off, and he got his share of orders from the black community.

Racism wasn't the only problem Ronny ran across in his siding-selling experience. Being Jewish, he had been the victim of racial slurs for most of his life. The experience made him far more tolerant of people that didn't fit Middle America's parochial racist attitudes.

Door-to-door selling is hard enough without the hassle of racist loan officers. Selling can be a soul-crushing experience of negative responses, slammed doors, and vicious dogs determined to tear you to pieces. It takes a special kind of person to survive the indignities of the cold-calling racket.

Once a loan was approved, an engineer, Thomas Hines, was sent out to measure the house properly. No one in their right mind would accept the half-ass measurements of the mostly illiterate sales staff. Ronny may have left school early to become a jockey but his interest in reading and his pursuit of knowledge made him the intellectual superior to most of his siding sales peers.

Once Hines got the proper measurements he would add the job to the ready-to-install list. The sooner Ronny's jobs were installed, the sooner he got paid. It was important where Hines put his jobs on the list. If you were at the top of the list you got paid first, if you were at the bottom of the list, you sucked the hind tit.

Hines liked Ronny so his jobs were almost always put at the top of the list. Ronny wanted to make sure Hines continued to favor his jobs so he approached him. "Tommy we want to thank you for looking after us."

"No problem Ronny."

"Listen, how about a nice night out on the town, all expenses paid?"

"That's not necessary Ronny, I look after you because you're a good guy and you aren't always hassling me."

"I insist. I've already made all the arrangements. This Saturday go to the Guard House Restaurant and Tavern, the one that overlooks the Lakeside Racetrack. Ask for Karen, she'll look after you really well."

"Geez Ronny, you shouldn't have gone to all that trouble."

"Tommy, I owe you. You just have good time and if I know Karen she'll make sure you do."

Everything was arranged. Ronny knew the Guard House well. It served good food and as an added bonus it featured two beautiful women that worked the bar. Karen was the best-looking woman Ronny had ever met. For Ronny's hundred dollars Tommy would get the services of Karen, and for another hundred she'd cover the food and booze. The investment of food, booze, and the personal services of beautiful Karen, guaranteed that Ronny's jobs would be at the top of the list for as long as he worked selling siding. At least that was the plan. But like horse racing, you can fix everything so you come out a winner, but if the horse decides not to co-operate, you end up losing your bet.

Ronny can't wait for Monday morning to ask Tommy how his evening with the lovely Karen went. When Tommy comes into the office Ronny asks him expecting an enthusiastic response. "So Tommy, did you have a good time on Saturday?"

"Oh yes, it was very nice, the food and service was excellent."

"Speaking of servicing, what did you think of Karen?"

"Karen… oh you mean the young lady, yes she was very nice, very friendly."

This was not the response Ronny expected. After all, for two hundred bucks Ronny expected VERY FRIENDLY, not just very friendly. He had to find out what happened. That evening Ronny goes out to the Guard House to see Karen. When he walks into the bar he doesn't have to look hard. Karen in a low cut tight mini dress that barely covers her essential elements comes marching across the room with fire in her eyes. When she gets to Ronny she looks him straight in the eye. "You little prick… what was that supposed to be, some kind of a joke?"

"What are you talking about? Didn't Tommy have a good time?

"I couldn't get him hard. I tried every trick in the book"

"He's gay?" asks Ronny.

"Queer as a three dollar bill. Don't you know fags don't get turned-on by women?"

"Women are one thing but you're something else. I swear... I had no idea the guy was gay. So... since nothing happened does that mean I get a refund?" Karen halls off and smacks Ronny right in the face. She wheels on her six inch silver stilettos and heads back to the bar.

A Family Values Pit Bull

Ronny knew enough to keep his mouth shut. If Tommy liked men and kept it to himself that was his business, nobody else in the office had to know. As long as Ronny's jobs kept landing at the top of the list Tommy could screw goats for all Ronny cared. About a week later Tommy brings a young man to work, he's little more than a kid, and he's the prettiest boy Ronny has ever seen. If you took a quick look, you'd swear he was just a flat-chested girl.

Tommy asks Ronny if he would take the kid around on his rounds and show him the ropes. Ronny had no choice but to agree. If he refused his orders would end up at the bottom of the list. Ronny's sale's partner objects, he's another enlightened member of Middle America's family values *klan*. "He's a fag!" I don't want him in the same car as me."

Ronny lays down the law. "Don't be stupid. He's a friend of Tommy's and after the fiasco with Karen we got to be smart. He rides with us and that's that!"

"I don't like it."

"And I don't give a shit what you like. He's riding with us. In any case don't worry about it, a few days getting doors slammed in his face and being chased by vicious dogs and he'll decide there's a better way to make a living."

And so the kid becomes part of Ronny's team. For the first few calls the kid just stands back and listens to Ronny as he works the homeowners, absorbing the pitch. After a few hours they come across a house with a gate and a sign that says 'Beware of the Dog."

Ronny says, "Okay kid you give it a try. Go call on that house with the gate."

The kid says okay and starts to open the door of the car. As he does, the biggest meanest German Shepherd Ronny has ever seen comes out from the backyard barking, snapping, and drooling with anticipation of fresh meat.

"You're not afraid of dogs are you?" Ronny asks.

"Nah, I like dogs," the kid says, as he steps out of the car and heads for the front gate.

Ronny's sale's partner leans over to Ronny, "I hope the kid's got insurance."

Meanwhile the kid walks slowly over to the gate where the dog is still barking and drooling like the zoo keeper just rung the dinner bell. He gets to the dog, bends down on his haunches and says something to the animal as he pats him on the head. The dog licks the kid's hand and sits. The young man opens the gate and walks to the front with the dog heeling beside him. He rings the bell and a woman comes to the door. She opens it and looks at the kid and his new dog pal in amazement.

"How the hell did you get in here?" she says. "That dog hates everybody, he even bites my husband."

The woman is so impressed with the kid that Ronny is able to close the deal in minutes. Ronny and his partner can't believe it. Anytime there's a beware the dog sign, they send the kid, and every time the dogs see the kid, they become as sweet and docile as puppies.

Ronny never took his car to work, he left it home for his wife so she could take the kids to school and do whatever errands needed to be done. Ronny's partner usually picked him up and drove him home but on this day he couldn't, so the kid volunteered to drive Ronny home. When they got to Ronny's place he invited the kid in for a drink and to meet his wife.

When they got near the house Ronny and the kid are greeted by Ronny's pit bull, Rogue, who immediately proceeds to bite the kid in the butt. Rogue was the only dog ever to bite the kid. It must have been a Family Values Pit Bull.

Crossing the border was never easy, unless your owner knew the Governor. Learn more in "The Fixer" - Rebel Seed Publishing

The Wrong Place At The Wrong Time

During the Vietnam War Ronny was racing in Detroit. At the time every young American male was subject to the draft unless they had a deferment. If you received a draft notice you had to report to your Draft Board in a specified length of time. If you didn't, the Military Police would track you down and haul your ass in to the closest processing facility. Ronny wasn't eligible for the draft because he was a Canadian with papers to work in the United States.

Ronny shared a cubicle with fellow jockey, Chester Cullen, from Lawrenceburg, Kentucky, home of Four Roses Straight Kentucky Bourbon Whiskey. Good-old-boy Chester wasn't all that anxious to pick up a rifle, so when he got his Draft Notice, he decided to report to Motor City Downs Racetrack in Detroit instead of his local draft board. The military takes a dim view of avoiding the draft, especially during wartime.

Ronny and Chester were sitting at their cubicle getting undressed after a race. Two large MPs storm into the jockey's room and grab Chester who was standing there in his underwear. They see Ronny and decide to grab him as well.

As they're cuffing the two jockeys Ronny objects, "What the hell are you doing?"

"Shut up or I'll gag you!" announces one of the MPs.

They cuff Chester and Ronny, not allowing either man to get dressed. Ronny is at least still wearing his white riding pants, a t-shirt, and boots. Poor Chester is just in his skivvies. They throw the two men in the back of an unmarked military police car and head downtown. Ronny tries to explain that he's a Canadian and that they made a mistake.

The one in charge, a Sergeant, tells Ronny, "If you don't shut up I'll put you in the trunk." Ronny shuts up.

They take Ronny and Chester to a Coast Guard Processing Station on Jefferson where Ronny is hustled in to a cubicle where a doctor and nurse are about to give him a physical.

"Doc, they've made a mistake, I shouldn't be here…"

"Shut your mouth or I'll have them throw you in the brig. Now drop your pants and bend over." Just then Ronny spots an officer walking by. He shouts out to the passing officer.

"What do you want?" he asks.

"I'm a Canadian, I shouldn't be here."

"You're a what?"

"A Canadian... the MPs made a mistake, they got the wrong guy."

The officer looks at the nurse and says, "Bring me the MPs who brought this fellow in." The nurse runs off and in few minutes the Sergeant and his fellow MP arrive.

"Did you bring this young man in?"

"Yes Sir."

"Did you check his identification papers?"

"No Sir. He was with another fellow we've been chasing for weeks."

"What the hell is a matter with you? He's a Canadian. What do you want to do cause an international incident?"

"Take him back to where you picked him up, check his ID, and apologize."

"Yes Sir, right away Sir." And so the Sergeant and his fellow MP took Ronny back to the track where Ronny showed them his passport and papers. They apologized and the incident was closed.

A lot of young men who went to Vietnam, never returned, and some who did return were never the same. One fellow jockey Mickey O'Hara was drafted and went overseas. He was given one of the worst jobs anyone in the army could have, tunnel duty. He was handed a knife, a pistol, and a grenade, and told to kill anything that moved.

These were suicide missions, but every time he went down into the tunnels, he managed to come back. Eventually he was sent home but not unscathed. His heroism was rewarded with a variety of diseases he contracted from coming in contact with Agent Orange, a defoliant the military used during the war. Ronny's escape from forced military service was lucky, but thousands of young American draftees weren't so lucky.

After all the dangerous situations Ronny had survived over the years, it would have been ironic if he was killed in a rice paddy fighting a war he knew nothing about, in a place he didn't belong.

Ronny was downright genteel compared to his friend Nicky Larsen. Learn more in "The Fixer" - Rebel Seed Publishing

Some People You Shouldn't Fool With

By any stretch of the imagination Ronny was one tough character but some of his friends could match him incident for incident in the shear *chutzpah* department. One of Ronny's best friends was Nicky, Lame Duck, Larsen, an ex rider, trainer, and all around badass. Larsen walked with a limp from being tossed out of a makeshift ambulance on the way to the hospital after a minor spill on the track. He could have just walked away except for the insistence of the paramedics on taking him to the hospital in the track's homemade converted hearse that ownership passed off as an ambulance. The incident resulted in Larsen's new nickname and a permanent limp.

Don't think that the accident tempered Larsen's penchant for doing whatever it took to get even for an obligation not fulfilled. When a car dealer refused to pay Ronny for a race he fixed, Larsen set his car on fire right in the middle of his driveway. As the car went up in an inferno of flames he called the car dealer and told him if he didn't have the money by the following day that next time he'd be in the car. Nicky didn't mess around; he went straight for the heart, groin, or wallet, whatever was needed to get the job done.

Ronny was staying with Larsen after both men were divorced. Larsen loved old westerns, especially the ones with John Wayne. He paid the cable company extra just to get the Western specialty channel.

One night Ronny and Larsen were sitting drinking and watching an old Duke duster when the cable went out. It was raining outside and some lightning had hit the main receiver for the neighborhood. Larsen tried to call the cable company but he had trouble getting through. Everybody in the neighborhood had the same problem so they were all calling at the same time. When he finally got through he was able to talk to a young lady that handled repairs, but she was less than helpful.

"I'm sorry sir, but the receiver was struck by lightning."

"Okay, so when can you fix it."

"Well sir it's an act of God. You'll have to pay to have it reconnected."

"Really," says Larsen, well can you give me God's address so I can send him the bill?"

The woman laughs but insists that if he doesn't pay to have his cable reconnected, they won't come out. But Larsen doesn't get mad. He just hangs up.

Larsen turns to Ronny and says, "Come on, we'll show these people exactly who they dealing with."

Larsen instructs Ronny to drive him around the neighborhood. Every time he sees a house with cable he instructs Ronny to stop the car. Larsen grabs a large industrial cutting shears out of his trunk and proceeds to cut every cable connection to every house in the area, including his own. The next day the repair people come out to reconnect the people who paid, but what they find is everyone's cable has been cut. Larsen calls the company and speaks to the same woman.

"So are you going to come out and fix my cable now?"

There's a pause on the other end of the line, then the woman says, "It seems someone cut everyone's cable."

"Really," says Larsen, "so I guess I don't need God's address."

"We'll have someone out to fix your cable this afternoon."

"Young lady… some people are not to be fooled with. Have a nice day." That was Nicky, Lame Duck Larsen.

Dually Noted

Nobody screwed with Nicky Larsen, nobody that is, who knew him, but if you misjudged this good old hillbilly country boy with a limp, you most certainly would end up on the wrong side of some costly consequences.

Nicky moved out to San Diego and got himself a place and a couple of nice horses that could run. Nicky had money squirreled away from all his wheeling and dealing so he was able to install his horses at one of the finest training centers in the area, the San Luis Rey Downs Training Center. Shed Row, the stable area at the center, consists of a series of barns where the horses are kept. Nicky had a habit of staying late to look after the horses. After everyone else had left for the evening

Nicky took them out of their stalls and bandaged them. When he was finished he'd rake the area.

An anal-retentive woman owner whose horses were a couple of barns down on the same Shed Row started yelling at Nicky for staying late, disturbing her horses, and messing up the area in front of her barn after she'd had it all tidied up.

"I'm going to report you," she yells.

"Go ahead bitch, but I wouldn't if I was you."

"We'll see about that," she bellows.

Nicky turns to Ronny and says, "This bitch doesn't know who she's dealing with."

The next day Nicky is called into the office and told a complaint has been filed. The woman complained about Nicky staying late and messing up her Shed Row area. He was told he'd have to leave the area by a certain time from now on. Nicky says okay, but it's definitely not.

A few days later Nicky points out to Ronny that the woman has a brand new Dually truck. A Dually is an ordinary pickup but with a set of double tires on the back. It enables the truck to haul bigger loads.

Nicky tells Ronny to feed the filly; he has something he has to do. Ronny watches as Nicky walks down to where the woman has left her truck. He takes out a knife and slashes the sidewalls of all four brand new tires. The tires immediately go flat and because he cut the sidewalls, they can't be fixed. A few hours later the cops show up and ask Nicky if he slashed the woman's tires. Nicky tells them he doesn't know anything about it and unless they have a witness or evidence that he did it, he has work to do.

They mention the yelling match the day before but Nicky says, "So what, that was yesterday, its all been straightened out."

He turns around and winks at Ronny. Since no one but Ronny saw him do it and they have no evidence against him, they leave. After the cops drive off, Nicky strolls down to the woman's barn.

She looks at him and starts screaming, "You son-of-a-bitch, you ruined my new tires."

He looks her straight in the eye and says, "Some people you shouldn't fuck with… cause when you do, things happen."

Nicky turns and walks away. From then on, he stayed on Shed Row as late as he wanted, and nobody ever complained again.

There is a difference between a hearse and an ambulance.
Learn more in "The Fixer" - Rebel Seed Publishing

The Almost Union

Ronny was riding for a Doctor who headed a syndicate that had twenty-five horses. It was a good gig as there was lots of work, but the owners were gamblers. Ronny would be instructed to hold a horse until the odds dropped, once the odds favored a good payday, they'd tell Ronny to let the horse run. In addition to Ronny's riding fee, the owners would place a two hundred dollar bet for him. It was a financially profitable arrangement, but it all ended badly.

It was a fall meet and the weather was terrible. Ronny was on one of the Doctor's horses in the third race and he was instructed to let it run, as the odds were perfect for a big score. There was snow on the ground and the track was treacherous. The first two races were disastrous with several spills involving multiple horses and jockeys.

The senior jockeys got together and voted not to race any more that day; it was too dangerous. To counter the jockey's boycott the stewards isolated the apprentice riders and told them they had to race or else. Names were put in a big jar and drawn to see which apprentice rode which horse.

The Doctor's horse ended up with a female apprentice who had never won a race. The horse should have won by five lengths based on the field he was up against, but the rookie jockey couldn't handle the horse and despite a lead going into the final turn, she lost by half-a-length. The Doctor was pissed. He confronts Ronny.

Ronny tells him, "Sure the horse should have won, and would have won if I was on him, but it was too dangerous. What if the horse went down and broke a leg? What if I got injured?"

"I don't give a shit," says the Doctor. "You get paid to take that risk. That's the job!"

"Not to get killed for a measly few bucks, it's not," says Ronny.

"You're fired!"

And so Ronny loses a good gig, but he's not going to take it lying down. The jockey's don't have a union but they do have a guild. A five-dollar guild fee is taken out of every jockey's paycheck per race: three dollars goes for hospitalization and two dollars goes for savings. Ronny calls the head of the guild who works out of New York, but the guild leader tells Ronny there's nothing he can do.

Ronny isn't happy. "So what the hell are we paying you for? I lost out on twenty-five good horses,"

"Look that's the way it is. It's just bad luck," says the guild boss.

Ronny had no intention of letting this go. He contacts the local head of the AFL-CIO. They're the union for the pari-mutuel operators, and Ronny's buddy Sal is the local shop steward. The head of the Michigan AFL-CIO wasn't a friend, but he was willing to go along if Ronny could sign-up the required number of jockeys needed to officially form a union. If the jockey's formed a union, they could go out on strike, and the pari-mutuel operators would follow in sympathy. That would close down the track.

Ronny and one of the other riders worked on signing jockeys up, but they came-up three riders short. Ronny went to the head of the AFL-CIO and asked if he could use Sal to get the signatures of the remaining three jockeys they needed, but the union leader said no. The next day Ronny sees his picture in the newspaper with an article about how he is trying to form a jockey's union with the help of the mob.

The stewards call Ronny in and demand he handover the union signup cards, and that he pack up his gear and get lost. He was no longer welcome at the track. Ronny called the head of the union who in turn called the track officials demanding Ronny be given back the cards and reinstated, or there'd be a lawsuit and a whole lot of trouble.

Since the pari-mutuel operators were already part of the AFL-CIO, the track didn't want any trouble, so they reinstated Ronny and gave back the cards. Unfortunately Ronny was still three signatures short of qualifying for union status.

The guild was angry with Ronny for his attempt to form a union and usurp their power and source of revenue. He was summoned to a meeting at a downtown hotel with all the senior guild officials from around the country.

Two FBI agents approached Ronny as soon as he entered the meeting. They wanted to question him about his so-called mob affiliation.

The head of the local chapter of the AFL-CIO intervened telling the FBI agents to get lost. It was a private meeting between the guild, Ronny, and the AFL-CIO. The union never did get off the ground, but at least they couldn't throw Ronny off the track.

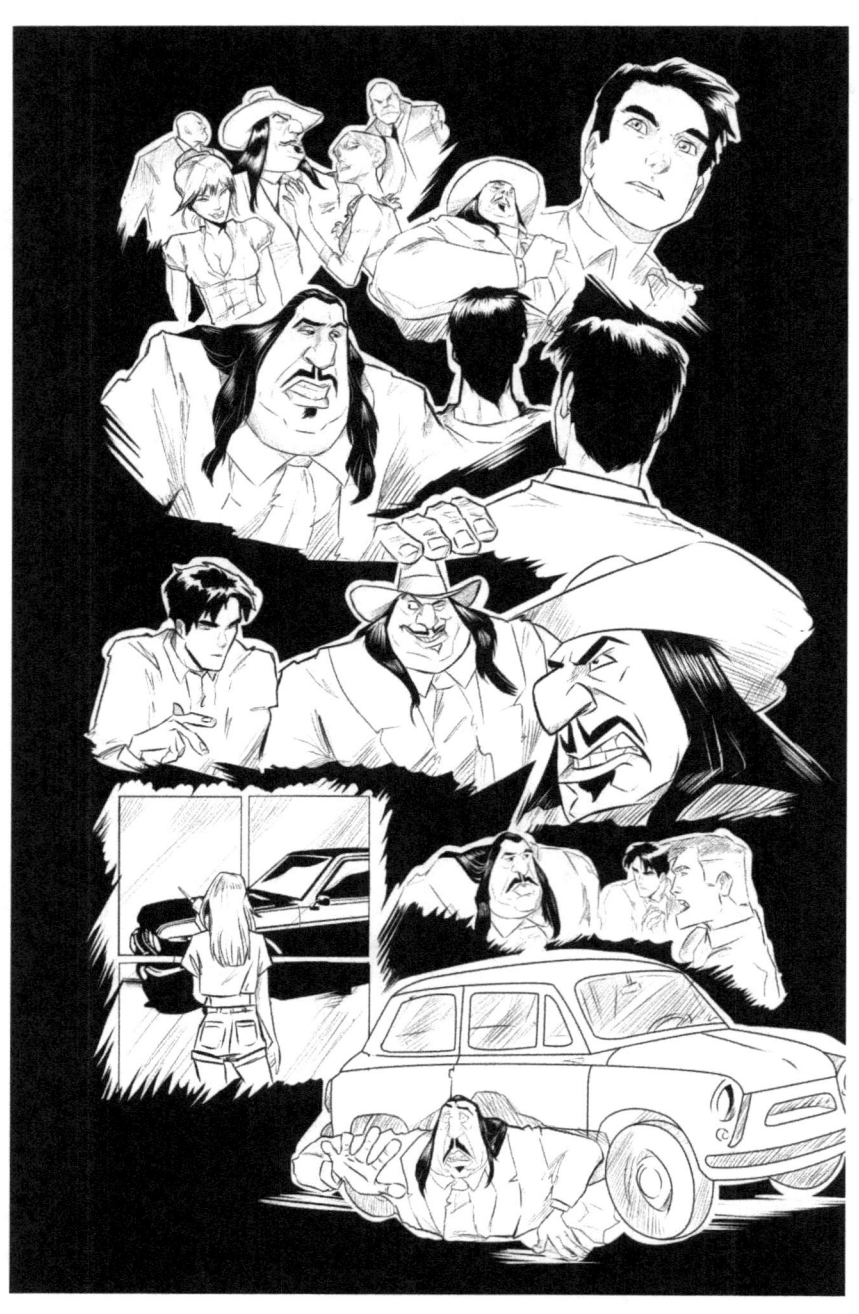

Nabo Polassar, King of the Chaldeans
Learn more in "The Fixer" - Rebel Seed Publishing

Part III

The Gamblers and Gangsters

Killer Chickens

Gambling is a basic instinct. It's primal. Everyone gambles on something: lotteries, poker, football, horse racing, and bingo. Even sweet little old ladies will lay down a dollar for a chance to win the prize-winning apple pie at the church picnic. It's all gambling and we all do it. Some would argue crossing a busy intersection at rush hour is a gamble, one you don't want to lose. We seem to need the rush, the excitement, the danger of losing, and the exhilaration of winning. People will gamble on anything, horses, dogs, camels, even chickens; to be more precise, killer roosters, or if you prefer, killer cocks.

Ronny's friend Nicky Larsen raised fighting chickens. It's a brutal, vicious excuse to gamble, to vicariously risk another living creature's life just to feel the thrill of the hunt, a throwback to our ancestors' days on the Savannah. The money aspect is almost secondary to the ritual re-creation of the kill. It makes horse racing, and all its ills, seem positively genteel.

Ronny arrives at Nicky's farm to see him sitting on the porch holding a .22 rifle in his lap. Ronny asks why.

"Somebody's stealing my chickens, but I'll show'em not to fuck with Nicky Larsen's birds."

"So what are you going to do?"

"You'll see." Nicky takes Ronny into the house where he shows him a drawer full of razor sharp, double-sided blades each about two and a half inches long.

"These here chickens know how to fight. You attach these blades to one of their nails and they become killers."

Larsen then goes out to the yard where he attaches the blades to his birds. The next morning when they wake up and check on the chickens, there's a decapitated hawk lying in the middle of the yard. The hawk took one gamble too many, and lost.

Nicky takes Ronny and one of his chickens down to New Orleans where cock fighting is legal. There, Nicky introduces

Ronny to a friend, Murray Daniels, the best killer chicken breeder in North America and Mexico. Contrary to popular belief not all Jews are lawyers or accountants, and neither do they control the banks, media, or Hollywood. If there can be a Jewish jockey, and there were a few, there can also be a Jewish hillbilly killer-chicken breeder from Tennessee. Murray looked like he just stepped off the set of the Beverly Hillbillies complete with wild hair, a rope for a belt, and ten thousand dollars cash in his pocket.

Murray drives Ronny and Nicky to a huge domed facility that houses eight chicken-fighting rings. The fenced-in rings are surrounded by crowds of spectators eager to place wagers with Mexican bandit bookmakers that control the betting. These refugees from a 'Kill Bill' sequel could be carrying as much as fifty or sixty thousand dollars, which answered the question why they were so heavily armed.

Nicky enters his chicken into a couple of fights and wins. Both Nicky and Ronny win their bets but when Nicky enters his chicken into a third fight, Ronny hesitates. "I'm sitting this one out. I don't like the look of that other bird."

"Aah… Don't be a pussy." But Ronny wants nothing to do with this nasty looking scar-face rooster with the double-edged dagger strapped to his nail.

Murray told Ronny that Nicky's chicken was a 'ducker' meaning the bird would duck down low and play dead. When the other bird flew up over his seemingly injured body, it would attack, and decapitate the challenger. Unfortunately for Nicky's bird, the challenger was experienced, and didn't fall for the tactic. Nicky's bird is killed. At least in horse racing the losers don't die.

One Crazy White Boy

Two black gamblers wanted to do some business fixing races in Cleveland, so they contacted Ronny. Their day-job was collecting for the Teamsters; in other words they were mobbed-up. Aside from their Teamsters' jobs and gambling business, they ran an upstate bar called the Pink Orchid. Since Ronny won a few races with a filly by the same name, he figured the relationship was auspicious. He was wrong.

At the time jockeys were getting five hundred dollar to fix a race but Ronny demanded fifteen hundred because the horse he was riding was the favorite. If he got caught holding the horse, he would get suspended and that would cost him more than the fix was worth. Eventually they agreed on one thousand up front and a piece of the action on the backend.

Ronny was experienced enough to keep the horse off the board and out of the money. They prearranged to meet after the race at a local bar to pay Ronny his share of the profits, but they didn't show up, stiffing Ronny what they owed him. The two gamblers had already left town.

The next season Ronny was racing in Akron, the gambler's hometown where they had their bar, the Pink Orchid. Ronny runs into the two of them at the local track. They act as if nothing happened. They invite Ronny for a drink at a bar near the track. Ronny goes to the bar and they shake his hand as if he's an old pal.

They buy Ronny a drink and continue to act as if they never cheated Ronny out of his share of the profits. They want to do some more business. Ronny figured there was no sense in causing a scene. If he made a fuss they would just disappear, and Ronny would still be out the money they owed him.

Ronny agrees to work with them again and they give him three thousand dollars to payoff the jockeys in an upcoming race. Ronny doesn't pay the jockeys; he just keeps the money. Of course the race doesn't go as planned. Since the two gamblers know all the jockeys, it was easy for them to find out if Ronny paid them. They call Ronny threatening him. They want to meet and they want their money back.

Ronny reminded them that they never paid him his share of the profits from the Cleveland race, and as far as he was concerned they were even. But the two gamblers weren't buying it. If he didn't pay up, they'd get him. Ronny told them he had a .45 automatic in his car and if he got to it before they got to him, he'd be the one still standing at the end of the day.

Since their initial threat wasn't working, they changed their tactic. They told Ronny they knew what he drove and one day he'd receive an unwelcome surprise under his car, a Summer Christmas Present, a euphemism for a bomb. A few days later Ronny goes out to his car and sees a brightly wrapped box with a nice red bow shoved under his car. It was empty, but later that day Ronny gets a call from one of the gamblers.

"See how easy it is to get to you."

"Maybe so," says Ronny, "but you better not miss, cause you'll only get one shot. It's just as easy for me to put a bullet in each of your heads. As far as I'm concerned we're even, so let bygones, be bygones, and together we can all make some money instead of wasting time fighting over past differences."

They agree, and tell Ronny to meet them at the Pink Orchid. Ronny wanted one of his friends to go with him for backup but nobody wanted any part of it. The bar was in a rough part of town and Ronny was going to stick out like a vanilla Oreo in a box of chocolates. When he arrived at the bar he was the only white face in the place but the two gamblers greeted him like a long lost relative. They bought him a drink or six while they discussed a new business arrangement.

When the meeting was over they said they'd never met anybody like him, and that he was the craziest white boy they ever did business with.

To which Ronny answered, "You just can't scare a guy like me. You got to understand I really don't care. That's just the way I am."

Ronny knew not to deal with dummies, even if they were the boss's son. Learn more in "The Fixer" - Rebel Seed Publishing

Two Cops, A Gangster, And A Hawaiian

That's not the only time Ronny had a run-in with the wrong people. While in Detroit he was approached by two black men who wanted to fix races. Ronny and the two men met for lunch where they pitched Ronny on a deal. One of the men carried a large attaché case that he didn't leave out of his sight. Ronny could tell from the bulges in their jackets that these guys weren't the kind of people you wanted to fool with.

He asked them why they came to him and they told him he was recommended by a mutual acquaintance. Ronny was skeptical since he didn't know them and suggested they meet the next day after he had a chance to check them out. They agreed and a meeting was set for the following day.

That evening Ronny called their mutual friend and was told these guys were legit, but he did have one last thing to say. "You can't fuck with these people Ronny... they're Chicago cops. If you screw them, no one will ever find your body."

The following day they meet at a booth in the back of a restaurant where nobody had a direct view of what they were doing. An arrangement was negotiated. Ronny was to receive ten thousand dollars to pay jockeys to hold six of the nine horses in the next day's seventh race. He asked for an extra twenty-five hundred just in case one of the jockeys was reluctant. If he didn't need it he'd return it.

The man with the briefcase opened it. Ronny could see it was filled with neat piles of bills each banded and stacked in equal piles. He took out two stacks of five thousand dollars each and dropped them on the table in front of Ronny. He then peeled off another twenty-five hundred from one of the other stacks. The two black cops wanted to know how Ronny would get them the names of the horses to bet on. Ronny told them he'd meet them at the track and hand them a program with the three names circled.

The first jockey Ronny approached was a Hawaiian named, Akoni Kalani. He had two gold teeth and he rarely turned down one of Ronny's fixes, unfortunately this time he said he couldn't do it. He was riding for an owner that was connected to the Chicago mob. He never knew until the last minute whether or not he was allowed to let his horse run, or if he was supposed to hold him. This owner was not someone you wanted to mess with. Screw up and you may wake up one day being lowered into Lake Michigan wearing nothing but a pair of cement overshoes. Ronny had a choice: give back the money or take a shot at handicapping the race. He definitely did not want to give back the money so he chose three horses for the trifecta and hoped he'd get lucky.

Unfortunately Kalani finished third in a photo finish busting the bet. Ronny was screwed. He calls his pal Sal who tells Ronny, "You really shit in your hat this time. These two guys are bad actors, I better come with you as back up."

But Ronny tells him no. If these two hard-asses spot Sal they'll think Ronny intentionally screwed them for sure. Ronny calls them and sets up a meet at the Troy Hilton, figuring they wouldn't kill him in such a high traffic public place. Before he leaves for the meet he goes home and hands his wife, Annie, twelve thousand of the twelve thousand five hundred that the two crooked cops gave him. He tells her if he doesn't come back by the morning, take the money and kids and get out of town because he's not coming back. He'll be dead.

He heads for the hotel and when he gets there he backs into a parking space preparing for a quick getaway. He gives one of the attendants twenty bucks and tells him to keep an eye on his car: watch for anyone coming around to mess with it. When he returns, he'll give the kid another twenty. The kid agrees. When Ronny enters the hotel restaurant the two gamblers are waiting in a booth in the back of the restaurant. They want their money back.

"I haven't got it," Ronny tells them. "I used it to pay the jocks."

"Empty your pockets," the briefcase man orders, and so Ronny empties his pockets on to the table including the five hundred dollars he kept in reserve. "You want me to take off my shoes too," adds Ronny.

"Don't be a smartass you little prick! We want our money by tomorrow."

"Well, it ain't going to happen," says Ronny, "I already told you I used it to pay the jockeys. These things happen. There ain't no sure-things in this business, that's why they call it gambling.

What the fuck you going to do? Shoot me in the middle of the Troy Hilton Hotel. Conrad will have a shit!"

The older gambler looks at his partner, "This is one crazy Jew!"

The briefcase man pulls out his piece and sticks it in Ronny's face, "Explain to me why we should let you live."

Ronny looks him right in the eye, "I really don't give a shit what you do. Kill me. It ain't going to get you your money."

The older gambler puts his hand on his partners arm lowering his gun, "Maybe we should start with the chink, see if that changes your attitude?"

"First of all he's Hawaiian, and besides I wouldn't kill him if I was you," says Ronny.

"And why not," says the briefcase man.

"Because... the old timer the Hawaiian rides for used to be a member of the Forty-Two Gang. His best pal used to be Frankie

Potatoes. You're from Chicago; you know what that means. It wouldn't be smart to knockoff his jockey."

"Can you make us our money back?" says the senior thug.

"Look I'll do what I can, but there's only a week left in the meet. I'll call you if the opportunity comes up."

Ronny never called. He left the Hilton, checked in with the car jockey that was keeping an eye on his Cadillac. The kid said nobody came near it, so Ronny gives him another twenty. He goes home and is greeted by his wife. As he walks in the door, she turns to him from the couch and says, "You realize you're playing Russian roulette, and you know how that can end."

"Sure I do, but you still got the twelve thousand, don't you?" Ronny heads for the bedroom. It had been a stressful day.

A Shot In The Ass

While riding in Montreal Ronny met a couple of Natives who owned a few horses. These men obviously had money, probably from smuggling cigarettes across the Canadian-US border, but Ronny knew enough not to ask. Ronny won a few races for these guys working some angles to make a little extra-legal cash. Nobody could just enter Native territory to go fishing without permission, but these men told Ronny he could go any time he wanted. If anybody made an issue out of it, he could use their names and they would look after any problems that resulted. They even gave Ronny a business card to use in case of emergencies.

So on his day off, Ronny packed up his fishing gear and headed off to the Reservation to fish. He spent the day fishing, relaxing, and drinking beer. After a while two unfamiliar Natives approached him. The taller of the two spoke first.

"Hay white-boy what the hell do you think you're doing?"

"What does it look like, I'm fishing."

The shorter of the two men pipes up, "This is Native land. You can't fish here without permission."

"Really," Ronny says, "I have permission."

"Not from us you don't," says the bigger man. "Hand over your wallet, you've got to pay a fine."

"Fuck you! You can shove your fine up your ass."

At this point the taller of the two men takes a run at Ronny but Ronny ducks under the charge. The attacker goes over Ronny and ends up landing splat in the lake. Ronny wheels around and catches the shorter fellow in the jaw with a haymaker knocking him flat on his ass. The other fellow who is now soaking wet manages to get back to dry land. He grabs Ronny from behind and yells at his friend to help. While the taller Native holds Ronny, the smaller guy starts wailing on him. He stops to catch his breath.

"Hand over your money if you want to leave here in a vertical position."

"Okay, okay," Ronny appears to have had enough. His nose is broken, and his jaw and ribs hurt like hell. "I'll give you what I got."

The man holding Ronny lets him go. Ronny reaches into his pocket and pulls out a couple of hundred bucks. The smaller of the two men grabs it out of Ronny's hand, and the two men start to walk away laughing.

As they walk away Ronny staggers to his car and opens the trunk where he always keeps a loaded double-barrel shotgun. He grabs the gun and starts after the two attackers. The taller of the two men looks back with a great big smile on his face; that is until he sees Ronny coming after them with a shotgun in his hand. The guy takes off running. The other fellow is too busy counting the money he took from Ronny to notice what's happening. When he sees his friend take off he looks back, but it's too late.

Ronny rests the shotgun against his sore chest and fires both barrels hitting the attacker in the ass. The force of the recoil knocks Ronny on his rear-end, but he gets up and goes to the smaller attacker who is rolling around on the ground moaning in pain. The other fellow is long gone. Ronny is standing over the guy with his shotgun pressed up against his former attacker's temple. The man is still clutching the two hundred dollars. Ronny doesn't say a word. He just bends down and takes the money out of the guy's hand, turns and leaves.

The following day when Ronny arrives at the track he finds four very large Natives waiting for him. They ask Ronny what happened on the Reservation. Ronny tells them the two men tried to rob him and he was just defending himself and recovering his money. They asked who gave him permission to fish on their land. Ronny hands the obvious leader the business card the Native horse owners gave him. The Native leader looks at the card carefully; he hands it back to Ronny.

"We apologize for the inconvenience Mr. Kleinberg, we will handle this matter and those men internally. Rest assured your shotgun pellets aren't the only punishment these two morons will receive."

Ronny looks at the leader of the group, "Yeah, inconvenience... I suppose that's one way to put it." The men smile and leave.

Sal makes Ronny an offer he had to refuse.
Learn more in "The Fixer" - Rebel Seed Publishing

The Cuban

Ronny's oldest son had a part time job at a local Ocala restaurant. Ronny would occasionally pop in to the place that was owned by a Cuban, Ricardo Moreno. His buddy and frequent protector, mob collector Sal Latorre from Detroit, told Ronny to look Moreno up if he ever needed anything while in Florida. So Ronny figured he'd make himself known from a distance.

Moreno's restaurant had a few pool tables and Ronny still liked to keep his hand in the game. He enjoyed playing, almost as much as taking money from wannabe redneck pool sharks that thought the little man was an easy mark. Moreno noticed how Ronny carried himself. He could see Ronny had been in his share of dingy bars and pool halls dealing with people who misread his size, underestimating his take-no-prisoners attitude, both on the track and off. For Ronny, there was no such thing as a friendly game; it's just not the way he was made.

On one particular evening Ronny was practicing his skills on the felt when Moreno approaches the table. He picks up the seven-ball just as Ronny was about to sink it in the corner pocket. "You ever notice how the locals think anyone who speaks Spanish is a drug dealer?"

"I don't judge. Everybody's got to make a living. What people do is none of my business, as long as it doesn't get all over me."

Moreno smiles. "I've seen you around. You like the t-bone with fries and vinegar, and you play a pretty good game."

"I'm pretty sure I paid my bill, what's wrong? Didn't I leave enough of a tip?"

The big Cuban laughs, "Nah nothing like that. I just wanted to invite you over to my place for dinner. Something I'd like to discuss." He places the seven-ball back on the table exactly where he picked it up. "Sally says hello."

Obviously Moreno had checked him out with their mutual friend. Ronny figures, what the hell, he was always up for a free meal; how bad could it be, the guy owns a restaurant. That Sunday evening Ronny goes to Moreno's house and has dinner.

Afterwards, they're sitting around sipping on some nicely aged whiskey when Moreno asks Ronny if he'd be interested in making some money. Ronny was never one to turn down extra cash, even if it obviously had some strings attached.

"Who do I have to kill?" Ronny meant it as a joke, but Moreno doesn't laugh.

"You leave that part to me, all you have to do is drive."

"That's all? Just drive?"

"Just drive that's all. Two thousand a day when I need you."

Two thousand dollars a day was too good to turn down, even if this Spanish-speaking wise guy actually did fit the local's prejudiced stereotype. Ronny starts driving Moreno around without incident. They become pretty close and Moreno even takes him to meet his parents and five brothers. His mother takes to Ronny immediately; she even shows him a picture of a young version of herself in fatigues, standing holding a machine gun beside Fidel Castro. Before they leave Ronny notices Moreno and his parents talking in the corner, with the occasional glance in his direction. There appeared to be nods and smiles that Ronny took as a sign of trust and acceptance.

What Twenty Thousand Buys

On the way back from Tampa one afternoon, Moreno tells Ronny that they have to go to Miami. It was an easy extra two thousand.

"What's up? Is there a problem?"

"Nah, nothing serious I just have to get my brother out of jail."

"Really? What's he in for?" Ronny asks.

"The feds found two kilos of cocaine in his house. Two kilos is intent to distribute. He's looking at twenty years."

'How the hell did they get a warrant to enter his house? I thought he never let anybody in his place?"

"*El es estúpido!* He's stupid. He reads an ad in the local paper for a new cleaning service: three rooms for the price of two. So he calls them up and has them come over to clean. But these assholes are Feds. As they clean, they check all the closets and find the coke. They take pictures and within two hours the house is surrounded, and Carlos is fucked."

"So how are you going to get him out of jail?"

"We're carrying twenty thousand dollars. And we're delivering it to a Congressman's son who happens to be a criminal lawyer."

"So what does twenty Gs buy you?"

"Two years probation. Not bad considering…"

It's Not Always Skeletons In The Closet

Ronny would drive Moreno up to Tampa at least once a week. They'd find some rural diner and make a call. They'd have breakfast and wait for someone to arrive. Shortly after they arrived, someone would come, exchange a few words in Spanish with Moreno, take Moreno's keys, and drive off with his car. Moreno and Ronny would have no choice but to sit and wait.

A couple of hours later another guy would show up and wave to Moreno in the restaurant. Ronny and Moreno would get into the new guy's car and they'd be taken some place else. Sometimes it was a house; other times it was a restaurant. It was never the same place twice. This would happen two more times until about six hours later the original guy would show up with Moreno's car and hand Ronny the keys.

"We're loaded," Moreno tells Ronny. "Drive slowly and don't stop for anything or anybody. Understand?" Ronny nods, acknowledging the importance of not getting stopped.

Ronny normally never asked too many questions. It was an easy two thousand bucks for six hours work, why complicate things with knowing what you were doing, even when you had a pretty good idea of what was going on. Everything ran smoothly without a hitch but Ronny did start to notice that Moreno's brand new SUV was leaking oil. Ronny tells Moreno there's something wrong with the car.

"Ricky, the car is leaking oil. We better take it into the shop."

"Nah, it's fine."

"But what if the car breaks down, I'm pretty sure you don't want any highway patrol cars stopping to give us a hand."

"The merchandise is in the panels wrapped in plastic. We drench the panels in oil to mask the smell so the police dogs can't smell it. Don't worry. We know what we're doing. You just drive." And that is exactly what Ronny did.

Sometimes Ronny couldn't help himself, he just had to ask questions. When he wasn't driving Moreno to Tampa he was sent to Miami for a pickup. He'd arrive at some suburban house, knock on the door, and be invited in by another Cuban expat. Once inside the house Ronny would be handed a large brown bag that he took back to Moreno in Ocala. This went on for three or four times until Ronny got pretty friendly with the

Miami connection. Now when Ronny arrived he was invited to sit down and relax before his long drive back. The Cuban would sit behind his desk and Ronny would sit in the chair opposite. Ronny noticed the guy was always alone. There was never another soul in the house.

He just had to ask. "So tell me, you're always alone? What's stopping someone from robbing you?"

The Cuban reaches under the desk and presses something. A second later another large Cuban comes out of the closet with a sawed-off shot gun slung over his shoulder aimed right at Ronny's head. "That's what stops them."

Half joking Ronny asks, "Has anyone ever tried?"

"Oh sure," the Cuban says, "he's buried out in the back."

Not Quite Routine

Most of the trips with Moreno were routine but on this occasion as soon as he gets in the car Moreno hands him a loaded .45 automatic.

"You know how to use one of these? Moreno asks.

"Sure," Ronny says, "I got one just like it."

"Good!" Moreno says, "You might need it. This trip could go sideways."

Ronny doesn't say a word. He's been in sticky situations more than a few times, but he always had Sal around to back him up. He trusted Moreno but when things go bad there's always collateral damage, and there was no way he was putting himself in the line of fire. Not for Moreno, Sal, or anyone else

When they got to where they were going Moreno instructs Ronny to stay in the car and keep the gun handy. "If anybody comes out of that house but me, it means I'm dead. If anybody approaches the car, shoot the bastard, and takeoff."

This didn't sound good. Driving drug dealers around was one thing, but getting in the middle of a shooting war was something else. About ten minutes later a good-looking black girl comes out of the house slinking her way down the street towards the car. Ronny is in the driver's seat. He picks up the .45 that was resting on his lap. The woman comes right up to the driver's side window. Ronny presses the button to lower the window.

"How you-all doing?" she says.

Ronny raises the gun, and jams it hard against the woman's temple. "Get the fuck out of here before I blow a big fat hole in your pretty little head. And tell your friends if anybody but my friend comes out that door… they'll be greeted by my two pals, Smith And Wesson. Now fuck-off!"

The woman takes off; this time not bothering to shake her ass on the way. Moreno comes out of the house and gets in the car. Ronny points to the woman reentering the house, "I almost shot that broad."

Moreno, "You should have."

A .45 always trumps a knife, no matter how big.

Learn more in "The Fixer" - Rebel Seed Publishing

Bobby The Bug Man

Jockeys are nomads that travel the country going from racetrack to racetrack looking for rides. These little men in the brightly colored silks live in the moment; long-term planning is a luxury most cannot afford.

They are independent entrepreneurs with a unique skill-set thrust upon them by size and a willingness to put their lives on the line four or five times a day. When you live in the moment you tend to burn through whatever money you earn, after all, what's the point of putting something aside for a rainy day when tomorrow could be your last. Jockeys are realistic, some would say fatalistic; they know nobody gets out of the business unscathed. Ronny was no exception.

So when things dry up it means you have to find other employment, even if it's only a temporary gig to tide you over until the next ride comes along. Ronny occasionally found himself in these situations.

When you travel in the circles that Ronny traveled in, you're bound to meet your share of oddball characters, and none was more interesting than Bobby The Bug Man. Bobby was this tall, good-looking redneck with long black wavy hair. He always dressed in black with a long black leather duster; he looked like he just stepped off the set of "Gun Smoke." He wore dark oversized aviator sunglasses and if you didn't know better you might have mistaken him for country singer, Ronnie Milsap.

Bobby was the greatest salesman Ronny ever met. He worked for a fellow that owned a large stable of horses and Ronny was one of his jockeys. The horse owner approached Ronny one day and told him he'd sold his horses and was going into the extermination business, not the same extermination business that Ronny's pal Sal was in, but rather the termite extermination business. Since Ronny was temporarily unemployed, the owner asked Ronny to come to work for him along side Bobby, the consummate salesman who couldn't read or write.

Unfortunately Bobby felt the hundred thousand dollars a year he earned planting termites in unsuspecting homeowners basements wasn't enough, so he went into the drug business. He offered Ronny a deal to warehouse his inventory but Ronny wanted no part of it. So he quit. It was time for Ronny to move on before he got caught in the middle of a fatal extermination. It's a good thing too, because Bobby The Bug Man ended up on the evening news after he and his Pancho Villa look-alike sidekick were killed in a shootout with the FBI during a drug raid.

Take Your Medicine Like A Man

Ronny and his wife Annie were just finishing dessert after having a nice dinner in a local restaurant. The waiter places a faux leather folder containing the bill on the corner of the table. A short, middle-aged, heavyset man in an expensive suit approaches the table. He takes an empty chair from a neighboring table without asking the diners and sits down between Ronny and his wife.

Ronny looks at the fellow. "Can I help you?" Ronny asks as he consumes the last bit of hot apple pie à la Mode. Ronny's wife stays silent.

"I understand you're the man to see if one wants to do some business." It's a statement not a question. "Come see me tomorrow and we'll talk."

The man reaches into his pocket and takes out a card; he slides it across the white linen tablecloth in Ronny's direction. "Make sure you present this card, or they won't let you in."

The man gets up, picks up the faux leather folder containing the bill, and heads for the front desk. He pulls out a roll of bills big enough to choke Seattle Slew. He peels off a few bills, stuffs them in the folder, and drops it on the front desk and leaves.

Ronny and Annie have been watching him the whole time. Ronny turns to his wife and says, "If I knew someone was going to pick up the tab, I would have ordered a more expensive bottle of wine."

The next day Ronny calls the number on the card. He arranges an appointment with the well-dressed, heavy-set bookie. The man owns a bar that caters to an assortment of heavies and their hanger's on. Two large scary bouncers greet Ronny as he enters. Ronny flashes the man's card and he's told to follow. Ronny is taken to a backroom office where the man is seated behind a large mahogany desk reading the local newspaper.

Images of racehorses and semi clad well-endowed ladies line the walls. The two thugs bracket the door. The man continues to read for a few seconds leaving Ronny stand. He puts down his paper and off-handedly waves at one of the two visitors' chairs that sit across from his desk.

He starts to talk. "We only do one race a day, never more than that. We only stop one horse, the favorite; it reduces the number of people who know what's happening. We don't need a bunch of stooges screwing up the odds. You know all the jockeys. You have a reputation of knowing how these things work. We're prepared to pay you a thousand dollars every time you make an arrangement. The jock gets two thousand for his efforts, or should I say for accomplishing the task. We usually have about thirty grand riding on a race, so this is serious business. If you or anyone else fucks us, there are consequences… terminal consequences. Do you understand?"

"Yes sir," says Ronny, "I ain't no virgin."

"So I've heard," says the bookie. "You interested?"

"The money's good; I'm interested."

"We'll call you when we need you." The bookie picks up his newspaper and starts to read. One of the thugs opens the door inviting Ronny to get out.

A few weeks go by and Ronny arranges several fixes. Each time Ronny is told which jockey needs to be approached. He's given three thousand dollars, two to payoff the jockey, and one for himself. After a month Ronny gets a call from the bookie.

Someone is bringing a horse up from Miami that's been running in five thousand dollar races. It's being dropped down to a twenty-five hundred dollar race meaning that it will most certainly out-class the rest of the field. The problem is none of the bookie's men can get to the jockey. He's too careful and just won't talk to anyone. The bookie wants to know if Ronny can get to him.

"Sure I can get to him, he's a friend of mine. He just lives around the corner."

Ronny is given the go ahead and the money to make the approach. In the evening before the race Ronny goes to see the jockey in his second floor apartment around the corner. The jockey agrees to the arrangement and Ronny gives him the cash. The jockey reaches for the cash but Ronny doesn't let go of the money.

"Take my advice. I've looked at the racing form and checked out this horse. There's no way you can hold him. I'm the best, and I wouldn't try to hold him. You got to come off the horse."

The jockey is cocky, "I can hold him, no problem, don't worry."

"Listen to me... these guys don't fuck around. You screw this up; you could get us both killed. Take your feet out of the irons in the gate and when the horse takes off, he'll leave you there. Don't be a schmuck; you're getting two grand to fall off the horse. That's the only way you'll get it done."

"Don't worry about it, I've held horses before."

Ronny is concerned but he lets go of the money. He thinks to himself, 'I hope this guy knows what the fuck he's doing."

The next day Ronny watches the race. The starting bell goes off and the gates open. The horse's head goes up in the air from the jockey's attempt to hold him. His head comes down and he fires out of the chute in sixth place. As they go down the straightaway a hole opens up like the parting of the Red Sea. The horse sees the opening and takes off; it passes the other horses as if they're standing still. The horse wins by a length and a half.

This isn't good. Ronny has to protect himself so he heads on down to the bookie's club to discuss the problem. When he gets there he explains that he paid the jockey and instructed him to come off the horse but the guy wouldn't listen. The bookie nods. He points to the two thugs standing by the door. "You go with these two men. Take them to this jockey's place."

'Hold on a minute... you're not going to kill him are you?"

"You know a better way to solve this problem. We're out thirty grand."

"You kill him the thirty grand is gone for good. Scare the shit out of him but don't kill him, use him, he's yours for free for the rest of the meet. You'll make back your thirty grand and more."

"Okay, you go and speak to him. If he agrees my associates will just rough him up a little. Teach him to follow instructions."

Ronny gets up to leave but the bookie stops him. "I want the thousand we gave you for the race." Ronny figured that was coming. He reaches into his pocket and takes out an envelope containing the money and hands it to the bookie. The bookie counts it and nods to the two thugs. The three men get into a car and head for the offending jockey's apartment.

When they arrive Ronny tells the two enforcers to wait in the car, he'll bring the jockey downstairs.

"You got ten minutes, if the guy's not down here by then, we'll come up and get him."

Ronny heads up the stairs to the jockey's apartment. He knocks on the door. The jockey opens the door and tries to hand Ronny the two thousand dollars. Ronny tells him that won't cut it. He has to go downstairs and talk to the two mobsters waiting for him.

"Are they going to kill me?"

"No but they'll probably rough you up a bit." Ronny proceeds to explain to the jockey his new obligations and how he negotiated his survival. The jock is still nervous and hesitant.

"What if I don't go down?"

"Your new bride is here isn't she?" The jockey nods. "Well if you don't go down, they'll come up here and kill you, me, and your wife, so let's be clear… Get your ass downstairs and take what's coming."

The jockey heads downstairs while Ronny waits with the guy's wife. They're gone about an hour, one of the most nerve-racking hours Ronny has ever spent. They promised not to kill him but they don't take losing thirty grand lightly. Finally the jockey gets home with a few welts and contusions but nothing fatal.

Thirty years later Ronny is living in a small Canadian town near the border. The town's major attraction is the local racetrack. Ronny enters a McDonalds near the track where a lot of jockeys and trainers congregate for breakfast. Two obviously old-time jockeys walk in. One of them is the jockey who thought he could hold the horse.

He spots Ronny sitting alone eating his Egg McMuffin. Ronny recognizes the guy immediately. The jockey and his friend approach Ronny. When he gets to the table he looks at Ronny, then turns to his friend.

"See this guy, he almost got me killed."

Ronny finishes chewing his last bite of breakfast; he takes a sip of coffee; and looks the guy straight in the eye. "If I knew you were such an asshole I would have let them kill you. Now fuck off, and let me digest my breakfast in peace."

Nicky had the perfect wife, she couldn't hear and she couldn't speak. Learn more in "The Fixer" - Rebel Seed Publishing

You Win Some And You Lose Some

During Ronny's racing days he rode for Frank Hadley who was a researcher for one of the big oil companies. Hadley looked like a retired schoolteacher, complete with bow tie, suspenders, old fashion rimless spectacles, and a tweed jacket with leather patches on the elbows. Twenty years later after Ronny became a trainer and was retired from racing, he bumps into Hadley at Motor City Downs in Detroit.

Hadley remembers Ronny from his racing days and he asks Ronny if he still breezes horses for their morning workouts. Although Ronny doesn't race any more he still breezes his horses; at the time he had two. Hadley asks Ronny to breeze his two horses and to let him know what he thinks of them. Ronny does and Hadley pays him twice as much as the normal fee for such a service.

Hadley tells Ronny he has to go out of town for a couple of weeks and could he look after his horses while he's away; he promises to make it worthwhile. Ronny agrees. When Hadley returns he thanks Ronny and pays him three times what it was worth to look after the horses. Ronny tells him it's too much but Hadley insists.

Hadley asks Ronny to dinner at Ginopolis', one of Farmington Hills fancier restaurants, a place with signed pictures of Sinatra, Muhammad Ali, and a wall full of Hollywood and sports celebrities. While at dinner, Hadley asks Ronny if he's interested in making some real money.

"I see you're just hustling to make ends meet. I know it's not easy after a divorce."

"You got that right," says Ronny.

"If you're interested I know a way you can make some real money."

"How legal is it," asks Ronny?

"It's a substantial amount of money. What do you think?"

"What would I have to do?"

It's easy if you like to drive. All you have to do is drive to Arizona and back. We'll supply the vehicle and pay all the expenses."

"The driving is no problem, but what will I be carrying?" It didn't take a wild imagination to figure out what the cargo would be, but Ronny asked anyway.

The kindly, old researcher, who liked horses and looked like a retired schoolteacher doesn't hesitate. "You'll be carrying two hundred thousand dollars on the way down and narcotics on the way back."

"And what's my end?"

"Ten percent, that's twenty thousand dollars."

Twenty thousand dollars was like winning the lottery. Ronny was interested, but he still wanted to know the risks. "Anything ever go wrong?"

"No, not really. If something goes wrong you just call this number." Hadley hands Ronny a business card with the name of a lawyer in Phoenix, and the slogan, "We make deals you're going to like… a lot!"

"You ever have a problem?"

"One time I'm half way across the country and I get a flat tire. The truck had just been reconditioned: new engine, new transmission, and new tires that were supposed to be puncture proof. I was sitting at the side of the road waiting for AAA to come with a new tire."

"Didn't you have a spare," asks Ronny?

"Sure I had a spare, but it was filled with two hundred thousand dollars. So as I was saying, I'm sitting there patiently waiting when a state trooper shows up asking if I wanted any help. 'No, I tell him, I'm waiting for AAA to come with a new tire, my spare is flat.' But the cop won't let it go. 'Let's take a look he says.'"

"I tell him not to bother, the motor league will be here any minute but he fucking insists. He takes the spare and tries to bounce it on the pavement but it won't bounce. He tries it again, and again it won't bounce. Before I could say anything he had me spread-eagled across the hood of the truck with my hands behind my back in handcuffs."

"So what happened then?"

"I just kept my mouth shut. All I said was, 'I want my lawyer.' I handed him the card and spent the next two days waiting. They'd cut open the tire and found the money of course. Finally this cowboy lawyer shows up, all decked out in a white Stetson, hand-tooled black and gold cowboy boots, and one of those suits with the fancy western stitching. He looked like a star from the Grand Ole Opry. He comes by the cell and winks at me. Twenty minutes later I was sitting in the front seat of his white Cadillac Eldorado on our way to pick up the truck."

"How the hell did he pull that off?"

"Like the card says, he made deals they really liked… a lot! He gave the cops half the money and we walked away free and clear. That was the end of it, just the cost of doing business."

A couple of days after Ronny's dinner with Hadley two Native Americans show up at the track. Hadley introduces Ronny to the principals of his little logistics operation. Unfortunately nothing ever came of it. Ronny figured there were only so many trips to be made, and perhaps it was a good thing to stay clear of, despite the potential profit.

Horse racing people are constantly on the move, traveling from venue to venue. No matter where Ronny was, Hadley seemed to show up. Ronny was in Kentucky buying horses. He'd already purchased a filly for twenty-five hundred when he saw a really nice black colt the owner wanted to sell for ten thousand dollars, but Ronny only had five thousand left in his kitty. The owner was in financial trouble having gone broke so he took Ronny's offer. That evening Ronny gets a call from Hadley who says he'll be there the following day and could he stay with Ronny. Ronny says sure and the next day Hadley shows up in his truck.

Ronny asks Hadley why he wants to stay with him, the accommodations aren't the best, but Hadley explains that his truck is loaded and he wants to keep a low profile. That evening they go out to a local tavern for a steak and some drinks. Hadley parks his truck right in front of the restaurant's big picture window so he can keep an eye on it. Ronny tells Hadley about the two horses he's just bought.

It isn't more than fifteen minutes later, a Sheriff's Deputy pulls into the parking lot and parks right beside Hadley's truck. Hadley gives Ronny a smile, gets up and goes over to the cop and starts talking. The cop has just come off duty and was stopping by for a quick drink before heading home. Hadley buys the cop a couple of drinks; they schmooze for about ten minutes, then the cop gets up shakes hands, and leaves. Hadley comes back to the table and as he sits back down, he says, "It's best to be sociable, you just never know when you're going to need a friend."

Later that evening, Hadley got deathly sick; he spends half the night in the bathroom throwing up. Hadley was not a young man and Ronny was worried the old man was going to croak on him. Ronny looks at Hadley who's sitting on the edge of the bed pale as a sheet.

"Not to be morbid or anything, Frank, but what happens if you die on me?"

"I die... I guess you get to keep the truck and the money."

"Fuck that," says Ronny, "I'll burn the truck and keep the money."

"Yeah," Hadley says, "that's what I would do." But the next day Hadley makes a quick recovery. Ronny never managed to land that big score but before Hadley leaves he asks Ronny if he wants to go partners on the two horses he just bought. He offers Ronny seventy-five hundred dollars cash for a half interest. Since Ronny only paid seventy-five hundred for both horses he figured it was a good deal.

A month or so later, Ronny is in Florida preparing the horses to race when Hadley shows up again. Hadley says he'd like to take the horses down to Tampa and place them with a trainer he knows but Ronny says no. Hadley counters with the idea that he'll take one horse, the filly, for himself, and Ronny can have the black colt.

Ronny knows the black colt is a much better horse than the filly. He figures the colt is worth about thirty thousand dollars and the filly is only worth about twelve. He tells Hadley that it wasn't fair; he'd be the big loser because the filly had long pasterns. The pastern is a set of two bones between the fetlock and the top of the hoof. A horse with long pasterns will not be able to take the constant pounding of racing on a regular basis and will ultimately breakdown, but Hadley always thought he was the smartest guy in the room, figuring he knew better. So Ronny reluctantly makes the deal.

Hadley runs the filly in three races, three weeks apart, and in the third race it bows a tendon; it's a rupture of the sheath enclosing the tendon that runs from the knee to the fetlock joint. A bowed tendon basically finishes the horse's racing career.

Meanwhile Ronny sells the black colt for thirty thousand dollars. Hadley tells Ronny what happened to the filly acknowledging that Ronny was right about the horse but he doesn't complain. He figures you win some and you lose some. He asks Ronny to keep an eye out for a couple of nice horses and to give him a call when he finds something. A few weeks later Ronny finds just what Hadley is looking for so he calls, but there's no answer. He keeps calling every day for a few weeks until he finally gives up. Hadley is either dead or in jail. Like the old man said, "You win some, and you lose some."

The vets had more tricks than a hooker on speed.
Learn more in "The Fixer" - Rebel Seed Publishing

Part IV

The Veterinarians and Trainers

Daryl, The Horse Doctor

Jockeys aren't the only screwballs in the racing business; the trainers and even the veterinarians indulge in their share of extra legal activities and bizarre shenanigans. One of the most colorful characters in the racing business was a close friend of Ronny's, Dr. Daryl Haddock. If Daryl was involved, you were more than likely going to end up embroiled in some crazy scheme or controversy. And if you weren't lucky, you might end up in jail. Take for instance the time Daryl called Ronny with a job offer from the Royal Family of Macao. The fact that Macao doesn't have a royal family, and is an Administrative Region of the People's Republic of China should probably have raised a red flag, but when opportunity knocks, Ronny is the first one to answer the door.

Daryl was going to be the veterinarian for some big shot in Macao and they needed an exercise rider. Daryl offered Ronny the job. It seemed like a good gig. All Ronny had to do was get on three horses a day for a thousand bucks a week. If you have cash in your pocket and like a good time, there was no better place in the world to exercise your proclivities than Macao, one of the largest gambling havens in the world. There is however a proviso, one must keep in mind, this little gambling oasis and it's kissing cousin Hong Kong, have very strict rules of behavior when it comes to horse racing, or horsing around in general. You're not in Kansas any more.

Daryl heads off to Hong Kong a few weeks early to meet a friend who's a member of a syndicate that owns a horse. In Hong Kong the rules regarding who can own, train, or even look after a horse are very strict. Individuals can't own racehorses. Only syndicates can own them. There are only fifty trainers allowed, and you can't become one unless one of the existing trainers either retires or dies. As far as veterinarians are concerned, they have to be off the track before the first race begins.

Daryl's friend was showing him around the track after the races had already begun. Daryl happened to have his medical bag of tricks with him, so when Daryl's friend showed him his horse, Daryl, who was an excellent vet, noticed the horse's knee was swollen.

Daryl offers to tap the horse's knee to reduce the swelling, a controversial procedure, but one that's done all the time. The problem with tapping is if you do it too many times, you weaken the knee, and basically condemn the animal to an eventual breakdown, ending its racing career.

Unfortunately for Daryl and his friend the tapping was done after the first race had already begun, a definite no-no in Hong Kong racing circles. When it was discovered what Daryl had done, he was told to leave the island immediately, and not come back. As for his friend, it turned out to be an expensive medical procedure. He was fined fifty thousand dollars by the Hong Kong racing authority. When Daryl got home he called Ronny in Florida to tell him that the gig in Macao was dead, as he was *persona non grata* in the region.

Daryl's Damaged Horse Power

Being around Daryl Haddock was like standing in the eye of a hurricane; you stood quietly by as Daryl careened from one disaster to another most of which he brought on all by himself. Take for instance the time Ronny visited Daryl after he had just bought a brand new BMW. They were at the track and as they were leaving they were watching someone trying to load a horse onto a trailer. Every time the grooms got the horse halfway up the ramp it got spooked, and backed right back down. This went on for ten minutes. The more they pushed the horse, the more anxious it got until the animal was so agitated it started to buck and flip. If the animal went off the ramp the wrong way it could break a leg and would have to be put down.

When a horse gets too anxious one of the best ways to calm it down without resorting to a tranquilizer is to blindfold it. It's like putting a cover over a birdcage at night. So one of the grooms goes and gets a large towel. They blindfold the horse so they can get it in the trailer.

Ronny turns to Daryl and says, "You better move your car. It's awful close to the trailer and there's no telling what that nutty horse will do."

"Fuck'em" says Daryl, "I'm not moving anything."

Meanwhile the horse is now completely blindfolded and the grooms start leading him up the ramp, but as usual this horse will have none of it. It flips backwards and comes off the ramp.

Now it's really excited and it starts running but it's blindfolded and can't see where it's going.

Everybody is yelling and running around trying to corral it, but all that does is make the animal more excited. It seems like the horse is running in six different directions all at the same time until it smashes into Daryl's brand new luxury BMW sedan.

Ronny turns to Daryl. "I told you, you should have moved your car."

To which Daryl replies, "Fuck you too!"

Disorder In The Court

One time Daryl was on his way over to Ronny's house late at night when he blacked out and hit another car. The cops were called but there was very little damage so Daryl and the other driver just exchanged insurance information. The cop warned Daryl to be more careful. Twenty minutes later Daryl blacks out again but this time it's on the highway and he rear-ends a tractor-trailer. Daryl isn't wearing his seatbelt so he is propelled through the windshield of his BMW. He ends up in the hospital badly hurt. His BMW is totaled. While in the hospital he is tested for a variety of sleep disorders but everything comes back clean. In the meantime the cops temporarily lifted his driving license.

Now Daryl has to go to court to try and get his license back, but since his license has been lifted, he needs Ronny to take him. They go to court and Ronny takes a seat in the gallery. Daryl's case is called and the Crown Attorney wants the female judge to throw the book at him. He demands that his license be revoked for a minimum of a year and that he be charged with multiple points. Daryl doesn't take the Crown's mock indignity well. He starts to yell and swear at him.

"Are you fucking nuts? How am I supposed to make a living without my license?"

"Well you should have thought about that before you got behind the wheel."

"Go to hell!"

Things were getting out of hand. The Crown and Daryl continued screaming at each other. Ronny who was sitting in the gallery can't stop laughing. Even the other members of the audience find the whole scene hysterical. Finally the judge has had enough.

"Quiet down you two, especially you Mr. Haddock. Behave yourself. This is a court of law and a certain amount of decorum is expected."

Ronny is laughing so hard that the judge notices. The judge points directly at Ronny, "Bailiffs throw that man out. If he doesn't go quietly arrest him; as for you Mr. Haddock, if you won't agree to the Crown's charges this case will have to go to trial. May I suggest an Arbitrator."

"An Arbitrator? What the fuck would he know?"

The judge has had just about enough. "This case is remanded for trial. In the meantime Mr. Haddock, your license is suspended."

The bailiffs escort Daryl out the door where Ronny is waiting. Daryl is hot. Ronny tries to calm him down but he can't stop laughing. An OPP officer, who is standing at the door of the courtroom, is looking at Daryl and Ronny. Daryl looks back at the cop and says, "What the fuck are you looking at?"

The cop looks at Ronny, "You better take your friend and leave before I throw you both in jail."

Daryl starts to argue but Ronny grabs him and hustles him out the building. When they get outside, Ronny is still laughing.

"What the hell's so funny, they took away my license and I got to hire a lawyer."

Ronny looks at his friend with tears of laughter in his eyes. "You're such a dummy, you can't talk like that in a courtroom."

"Yeah, well wait till next time…"

"Next time? There ain't no next time my friend, cause I won't be driving you anywhere, least of all to a courtroom. I almost got thrown in jail just being with you."

Like A Bee Is To Honey

Daryl Haddock was to trouble what a bee is to honey: if there was the slightest possibility of things going off track, Daryl guaranteed it would happen. According to Daryl, rules were for other people, not for him. As a horse doctor, he saw the rules of the racing establishment as mere suggestions, and his attitude toward society's rules were just about the same.

Understand... Daryl wasn't the only veterinarian that bent the rules in order to gain an advantage on the track. In fact some might argue it's part of the job description. But most other veterinarians know enough to play it straight when they're out of their own environment.

Daryl was working for a woman whose horse needed a shot of Lasix. Furosemide or Lasix is a heavy duty loop diuretic used to treat horses for pulmonary hemorrhages. When horses are worked hard they bleed, and Lasix is the common treatment, but the only people who can give a horse an injection are licensed veterinarians, not owners, trainers or anyone else.

If an owner or trainer gets caught giving a horse an injection, even if it's legal, they'll get ruled off the track for sixty days. You don't even want to get caught with a syringe in your possession because you'll suffer the same consequences. Of course Daryl doesn't care. He wanted to get home early, so he hands the owner a syringe of Lasix and tells her to inject the horse herself. And as you probably have already guessed, she got caught.

The woman feigned ignorance of the rules and told the stewards she was just following Daryl's instructions. Daryl was called in to explain himself and for the most part he managed to weasel his way out of trouble, but he was still fined five hundred dollars. Daryl, being Daryl, refused to pay. The stewards were not going to just let it slide, so they raided his truck in the middle of the night, and took all his medical equipment and supplies. He was hot. Finally Daryl's brother Sydney stepped in, and calmed him down and got him to pay. If he wouldn't have paid, the stewards were going to rule him off the track. If you can't get on the track, you can't work.

Oh Brother!

Daryl's cavalier regard for the rules was like a massive hurricane that leaves a path of destruction in its wake; friends and family were not immune from becoming collateral damage. Daryl and his brother Sydney were in Buffalo having dinner in a nice local restaurant. Daryl of course parked in a 'No Parking Zone' despite his brother's warnings.

"Daryl you shouldn't park here, you'll get a ticket."

"Fuck'em, what are they going to do, throw us in jail for parking illegally? Come on let's eat."

So Daryl and his brother go into the restaurant and enjoy a nice steak dinner. When they come out, they see a large heavyset cop putting a ticket on Daryl's windshield.

"Hay cop, what the hell do you think you're doing?"

"You can't park here, it's a 'No Parking Zone.' Didn't you see the sign? You're parked right under it."

"Fuck the sign and your ticket."

"Listen Mister, I'd watch what I say if I was you." And the cop starts to walk away. Daryl turns to Sydney and says just loud enough for the cop to hear.

"Look at that lard-ass... the way he waddles down the street."

The cop turns, "One more word out of you and I'll throw your friend in jail."

"He's not my friend, asshole! He's my brother." And with that the cop wheels around shoves Sydney up against the car, cuffs him, and hauls him off to jail. Daryl had to follow the cop to the police station so he could bail his brother out.

Daryl Versus Tesio

Ronny may have lived on the edge his whole life but he also knew when to back off. As a jockey involved in fixing races or in his dealings and relationships with gangsters, Ronny knew when to cut his losses. Daryl Haddock was a horse of a different color. As a side-note the expression 'a horse of a different color' goes back to medieval racing tournaments. People would bet on races even back then. The only way you could tell which knight was yours was by the color of his horse, and if you lost, you were told the winner was a horse of a different color.

Back to Daryl Haddock. He was definitely not your average veterinarian. In an occupation of colorful characters willing to bend the rules, Daryl was by all measure in a class by himself. In fact, one could say the guy was crazy.

Compared to Daryl, Ronny was the soul of discretion; where Daryl was a university educated veterinarian, Ronny was a self-taught athlete; where Daryl saw himself as a badass wise guy, Ronny was a badass who knew his limits; but despite their differences they were great friends. In fact when Ronny's racing days were done he and Daryl bought a horse, *Trés Vite*, together for thirty-five hundred dollars. Although Ronny wasn't racing any longer he still breezed horses and broke them so they'd be ready to race or sell.

Ronny started working with *Trés Vite* and found the horse could run, but it was unstable. In Ronny's words, "the goddamn horse is wacko." *Trés Vite* had a bad temper, was uncooperative, and downright squirrelly on the track. Ronny figured if he kept getting up on this nut case he'd end up getting hurt or killed. After all he wasn't as young as he once was, but Daryl thought the horse was the next coming of Whirlaway.

Despite Ronny's early exit from the public school system, he did go to the University of Florida at Gainsville to take courses in thoroughbred horse breeding where he learned about the Tesio Method. Federico Tesio was an Italian horse breeder, born in 1869, who developed a series of statistically proven breeding practices that are still in use today. The man was regarded as a genius and was responsible for five champion horses out of a stable of fifteen broodmares. His success rate in breeding champions is unparalleled with the descendents of his line, including the super stud Native Dancer, still dominating the world's racing circuits today.

It was with this knowledge of breeding characteristics and temperament that led Ronny to investigate deeper into *Trés Vite's* genetic background. What he saw wasn't promising. Despite the fact his ancestors had produced the occasional winner, they more often than not produced whack-jobs that drove owners nuts or caused mayhem wherever they raced.

Ronny knew Daryl was in deep denial about *Trés Vite*. Ronny figured he'd found a way out when an agent offered to buy him for thirty-nine thousand dollars. The horse only cost thirty-five hundred so there was a substantial profit to be made. When Ronny told Daryl about the offer, Daryl refused to sell.

"This horse is a winner. It will make us a fortune. Why sell it for peanuts?"

"Listen Daryl, I looked into this horse's background. And it isn't good. The horse is crazy just like its ancestors and it will cause us nothing but trouble. We can make a nice profit and use the money to buy a good horse."

"What the fuck do you know? I went to university. I'm a vet. You're a high school dropout who shovels shit in a barn all day."

"You know what Daryl, you keep the horse. You can have my share. Just don't ever come near me again. You're as fucking loopy as that dumb horse you love so much."

At that point Ronny walks away and didn't talk to Daryl until he was on his deathbed.

Dr. Dubon knew every trick, and invented many of them.
Learn more in "The Fixer" - Rebel Seed Publishing

Who Owns The Moral High Ground?

Ronny was good friends with one of the best, if not the best, veterinarians in the business, Dr. Dubon. Ethics and horse doctors are two concepts that probably shouldn't be mentioned in the same sentence. It's a fact of life that when there's big money on the table, moral principles often as not take a back seat to winning, even in the rarefied atmosphere of international stake races. Dubon was all about winning, and he had more ways to get a horse across the finish line first than just about any other individual in the racing racket.

It's not that Dubon didn't have ethics, he did; they just never got in the way of a big payday. Onetime he used his bag of tricks to cash thirty thousand dollars; we know this because Ronny was part of the play for which he received his small share, with the majority of the winnings going to a Nun who ran a Catholic Orphanage. It's that kind of moral ambiguity that both plagued and inspired the Doctor Feel Good of horse racing.

What Dubon never really got a handle on was the politics of horse racing. High stakes racing in the United States is an old-money Southern Gentlemen's Club. To this day the *nouveau riche* might be let through the clubhouse door but if you look closely, the modern day plantation owners are standing far away, holding their noses.

Ronny had no illusions: he like Dubon may have straddled the social layers as necessary evils to be endured in order to keep the mint juleps flowing, but everyone outside the inner circle had their tolerance quota, something Dubon never understood.

Dubon called Ronny with a job offer knowing Ronny was always eager to make some money, even if the circumstances required him to stretch, if not completely erase the line between legal and illegal activities.

"Ronny, I have a job for you if you're interested."

"Doc, you know I'm always interested in making a few bucks. Where's the job?"

"Saudi Arabia."

Ronny starts laughing, "Doc, how long have you known me? You know my last name is Kleinberg."

"So what? We'll change it."

Ronny is amused at Dubon's rather naive perspective, "Thanks for the offer Doc, but they'll never let me in the country. And even if they did, I'm pretty sure I wouldn't make it out alive."

That wasn't the only time politics and Dubon mixed to form an unfortunate cocktail with a bitter aftertaste. Dubon was working for a wealthy Northerner who had a horse that had a shot at a major stake race. We're talking about one of the big ones. Two weeks earlier the horse had won a prestigious race that was preparation for the real prize.

Unfortunately when Dubon took a look at the horse, its ankles were so sore it could hardly walk let alone run. Competing for a major title seemed out of the question. If the horse was going to run, something had to be done.

A week before the race Dubon, with the knowledge of the trainer, gives the horse a substantial amount, about 40ccs, of *phenylbutazone*, more commonly called bute. It's nothing more than glorified aspirin for horses. It reduced the pain and swelling in the animal's ankles but at the time its use was highly restricted. The bute was given to the horse six days before the big stake race, enough time for the drug to be eliminated from the horse's system, avoiding any undo issue with the urinalysis required of the winner. The race goes off and the horse wins. The testing process of the horse's urine seemed to take an unusually long time, but life goes on.

The timing couldn't have been worse. The United States was going through an historically unsettling time, particularly for the old South that somehow felt it their duty to keep on fighting the Civil War. It was the height of the civil rights confrontations of 1968.

Martin Luther King had just been assassinated by James Earl Ray, a racist bigot who excused his murderous antisocial actions with a flimsy veil of patriotic anti communist nonsense. The liberal northern horse owner felt he should do something, so he donated the winnings of the prep race to Coretta Scott King so she could continue her husband's work. This did not go down well with the southern racing establishment.

The northern horse owner became *persona non grata* at the track and his mailbox quickly filled with hate mail, and not just from the so-called crazy fringe. Even the so called aristocratic southern racing establishment types felt obligated to extract their pound of verbal flesh.

Low and behold, shortly after the horse owner's generous donation, the results of the urinalysis were released. Small traces of bute were reportedly found. The horse was relegated to last place and a new winner was crowned, depriving the northern liberal owner of the purse, and the prestigious trophy and title.

Ronny may not have received a formal education, but he is well read and has even taken university classes in horse breeding in order to prepare himself for a post-racing career in pin hooking. Pin hooking is an archaic term that comes from the tobacco business that is also used in the sale of livestock, including thoroughbred racehorses. Buyers purchase young horses and prepare them for sale based on their potential to win and earn money.

Pin hooking is the only real way to make money in the racing business. In any case, Ronny was always eager to pick Dubon's brain about whatever tricks or treatments he could learn. Years after the incident Ronny asked Dubon about what really happened and if the bute actually was the reason the horse won the race. What Dubon said surprised Ronny and maybe even shocked him.

"Bute is just an aspirin. That horse was in such bad shape no amount of bute was going to help it win anything. I gave it to him just to make him more comfortable."

"So how was it able to win the race?"

"What I gave the horse starts with an "H" not with a "B".

Ronny scratches his head, "But they never tested for heroin. According to the records they disqualified the horse for having too much bute in its system."

Dubon shows a rare flash of anger, "Bullshit! Those southern crackers didn't want some liberal Negro-loving northerner donating money to what they regarded as a bunch of colored upstarts who didn't know their place. That's the real reason the horse was disqualified. If one of their own owned the horse, everyone would have just looked the other way. They had no idea that the reason the horse won was because I gave it a shot of H. So you tell me, who really owns the moral high ground."

Horses with bad teeth and counterfeit ministers.
Learn more in "The Fixer" - Rebel Seed Publishing

Not All FBI Agents Are Mormons

While in Pennsylvania Ronny was doing some business when a new trainer came to town with some pretty good horses. The trainer worked with his daughter who was a jockey. Ronny approached the young woman and asked if she'd be willing to hold a horse. The jockey tells Ronny she'll have to speak to her father. So Ronny arranges a dinner meeting with the trainer. Despite Ronny's reputation as a wild and crazy guy he was always very careful about people. If you were going to be involved in extra-legal activities you had to trust the people with whom you were doing business.

Ronny picks up the trainer and they head out to the restaurant for some steak and a few drinks. On the way Ronny takes a tight corner just a little too fast in order to jostle the trainer to see if he was wearing a wire. He seemed to be clean. They have their steaks and talk about the upcoming race. Ronny propositions the trainer promising him the equivalent of the winner's share, to be paid the following day in cash, if his daughter holds his horse. The trainer thinks for a second before he replies.

"Yeah I could be interested, but I want to talk it over with my wife." The hairs on the back of Ronny's neck stand straight up. A cold empty feeling invades his gut. He feels sick. This guy is either a fool or an FBI informant. You just don't do that kind of stuff. It puts everyone involved in danger. If the wife gets pissed at the husband and she squeals to the Feds, everyone will end up in jail.

The next day Ronny goes to the track making sure he doesn't take the money he promised the trainer. When he gets to the jockey's room he's told he has to report to the steward's office. Now Ronny knows the guy is a rat. When he walks in the head steward is behind his desk with two FBI agents flanking him. They tell Ronny they received a complaint from the trainer who claimed Ronny approached him about fixing a race, and he was going to pay him today. Ronny tells the agents he doesn't know the trainer and he has no idea what he's talking about. They ask Ronny how much money he has on him? Ronny empties his pockets onto the steward's desk. He looks down at the few wrinkled bills and loose change.

"Think I can fix a race for eighteen dollars and thirty-five cents?"

"Why would this guy lie to the FBI?"

"I don't know, but I can think of at least two reasons."

"Like what?" asks one of the Feds.

"Maybe I beat this guy's horse somewhere down the line, or maybe I accidentally bumped his horse in a race, and the guy's held a grudge ever since."

"What's the other reason?"

"I'm a Jew. Maybe this guy doesn't like Jews."

One of the FBI agents comes around from behind the steward's desk and bends over so he can look Ronny in the eye. As he does he reaches under his collar and pulls out a *Magen David (A Star of David)*.

"You should know jock, contrary to popular belief, not all FBI agents are Mormons. Your ass is mine, so you better watch your step."

Mission Accomplished

The rest of the day passes without incident. Ronny leaves the jockey's room heading for the parking lot where his midnight blue Caddie is sitting waiting. As he approaches the car, a black sedan pulls in front of him. The window rolls down and the familiar stone-faced head of Anthony Biaggio's favorite *torpedo* appears.

"Get in!"

It's not a request. Ronny knows enough to follow orders. He gets into the back of the black sedan pushing in beside another of Tony B's stoic associates. The sedan pulls out of the parking lot and heads downtown.

"Tony B wants to see me?" Says Ronny. The two *goombahs* don't answer.

They drive in awkward silence for the next twenty minutes, finally stopping in front of 'Tony B's Original Deep Dish Pizzas." They park beside a "No Parking" sign that someone cleverly appended with "And That Means You Dummy." The driver stays in the car while the two mobsters escort Ronny into the pizza parlor.

Sitting in the back of the restaurant devouring a large plate of spaghetti and meatballs is Anthony Biaggio an elegantly dressed middle-aged man. His dark blue chalk-stripped suit stretches against the strain of muscles slowing turning to fat from an overindulgence of pasta, meatballs and Italian sausage. His bright yellow silk tie is perfectly set-off by the dark blue of his custom-made shirt. His teeth gleam like a brand new package of Chiclets. He has just the right amount of silver in his thick head of hair to denote a man well invested in his substantial image.

"Sit my friend, have something to eat?"

"No thanks, Mr. B. I'd love to but you know… I got to keep the weight down."

"Bullshit, I insist," Tony turns to one of his body guards, "Marco, tell Gus to make my friend some spaghetti and…"

"I really can't Mr. B, it's a weight thing." Says Ronny.

"Sure, sure, I get it. Marco, tell Gus to bring Ronny just the meatballs, forget the pasta. Jockeys, got keep their girlish figures, isn't that right Ronny?"

"Sure Mr. B, that's the way it is."

"Speaking of the way it is, this prick trainer and his daughter gotta go."

"Ah... Mr. B., it's not for me to tell you how to run your business but..."

"Fucking right it's not!" Says Tony.

Marco drops an enormous plate of meatballs onto the table in front of Ronny. Ronny looks at the plate of food and then at Tony.

"If you remove the trainer and his daughter from the picture it will come right back to me, and that wouldn't be good for either of us."

"Well something has to be done, my friend, this cannot be left unsettled. It's not just me you understand, there's the jocks, and other people… friends of ours who lost out on a big payday because of this shit-head. Lessons have to be learned."

"I get that," says Ronny, "leave it to me. I'll make sure they get the message in a way that you'll appreciate, and they'll understand."

"Okay Ronny, I'll leave it to you, now try some of those meatballs."

"Really, I can't…"

"Try the fucking meatballs!"

The next day Ronny is up on a horse in the fifth race. The trainer's daughter is scheduled for the same race on a horse that outclasses the field. This horse can really run and should win by several lengths. Ronny has let the word out to the other jockeys that the trainer's daughter isn't to finish the race, Mr. B's orders.

The race goes off without incident. Ronny and Phil Curry are neck-and-neck with the trainer's daughter coming up fast on the inside as they make the turn for home. Ronny and Curry are dueling for the lead in the middle of the track. The trainer's daughter sees an opening along the rail and she begins to make her move.

Ronny looks over at Phil and shouts, "Box the bitch! Now!" Curry moves to the inside just as the trainer's daughter whips her horse urging it to run. Ronny drops back one length boxing the training's daughter in. She has no place to go. Curry closed the opening along the rail and Ronny is blocking her move to the outside. She has no choice but to pull back and slow her horse, but she can't. She's not strong enough to handle the horse once it's hit full speed.

She's screaming and yelling for Curry and Ronny to get out of her way, but they hold their ground. She pulls on the reins with everything she's got but the horse won't slow down. The trainer's daughter is shouting obscenities but with no place to go, she's fucked! Her horse clips heels with Curry's horse and goes down. She's thrown into the rail landing hard on the track.

She has a broken arm, concussion, and a variety of other injuries. The horse is banged up as well; both will be out of commission for months. Mission accomplished.

Get Out Of Town And Don't Come Back

Ronny is screwed. It's time to get out of town, and as it happens he has a job offer in Cleveland. He tells his wife to pack up, they're leaving town. Ronny and his wife start heading out when Ronny tells his wife to turn around.

"What's wrong? You forget something?"

"Nah, we can't leave yet."

"Why? What's up? I thought they didn't have anything on you?"

"Head to the Federal Building, I want to make sure. The last thing we need is for the FBI to come looking for me in Cleveland."

They pull up in front of the local FBI office and Ronny tells his wife to wait for him in the car. He goes into the building and approaches the receptionist's desk. He tells the clerk his name and he asks to speak to the person in charge of the case. A few minutes later he is ushered into someone's office. The agent greets Ronny like he's a long lost friend, offers him a seat, and some coffee. Ronny declines saying he won't be staying long. The agent obviously thinks Ronny is there to confess and to turn-in his gambling associates for a free pass.

"So Mr. Kleinberg, what can I do for you?"

"I'm on my way to Cleveland for a job. I want to know if you think you've got anything on me, and if you plan to come after me in Cleveland." The smile on the Agent's face disappears. He leans forward; he extends his arms onto his desk. He needlessly rearranges some pencils and papers seemingly for dramatic effect.

"Mr. Kleinberg... Have a nice trip." Ronny gets up and turns for the door.

"Mr. Kleinberg..." Ronny stops and turns to look at the agent. "Have a really nice trip, and do us both a favor, don't come back!"

When Ronny heard a friend's ex was beating her, he called Bats.
Learn more in "The Fixer" - Rebel Seed Publishing

Running A Ringer

Doctors Dubon and Haddock were not the only veterinarians who played fast and loose with the rules. In fact it is more likely to find a vet that is soiled around the edges, than it is to find one that's squeaky-clean. Most veterinarians that get caught are suspended for various lengths of time, and occasionally one will get banned for life, but every once in a while somebody ends up in jail.

Ronny once worked with a veterinarian that almost got away with one of the biggest switcheroos in the history of horse racing. The vet purchased two horses from Argentina that looked exactly alike; both were jet black with a small cowlick or hair whorl on their necks. One horse was a dog that never won a race; the other was a champion with ten wins in South America under his belt. At the time Argentina did not tattoo horses for identification purposes. Starting in 1947 North American racehorses have been tattooed on their upper lip with the identification linked to their registration papers, but this practice had not worked its way down to South America.

When the horses arrived, the second rate horse, a maiden that had never won a race, was entered into a couple of races under the name of its champion doppelganger. The horse finished last in both races. The vet then entered the champion into a sixteen thousand dollar claiming race, assured that no one would claim him because of his supposed poor showings in the two previous races.

The races were being held at one of New York's bigger, more prominent racetracks where the veterinarian's substantial ten thousand dollar bet was hardly noticed, and most likely had little or no effect on the odds. The horse went off at 80:1. It won by five lengths providing a substantial windfall for the crooked animal doctor.

No one was the wiser for two years. The vet was home and cooled out; that is, until he and his wife had a falling out that most likely involved a pretty two-legged filly that the doctor was riding in his spare time. The wife knew all about the scam her husband pulled. She went directly to the FBI as soon as the ink on the divorce papers was dry.

The vet ended up in jail. Nobody knows how many times this kind of stunt has been successfully completed, but there are a few documented incidents where the switch wasn't good enough. To paraphrase the old expression, 'close only counts in horse shoes, not horse racing.'

Punch Drunk Agent

At one time Ronny had an agent by the name of Lefty Milton Fitzgerald, a six-foot five-inch monster of a man with the body of a twenty-year old George Foreman, and the face of a ninety-year old Daryl Trjeo. His nose was broken so many times it could pass for a topographical map of Lombard Street in San Francisco. His ears looked like two misshapen cabbages attached to the side of his head. None of this was surprising as Lefty Milton Fitzgerald was an ex boxer.

Lefty looked like one of the scariest people you'd ever meet, but in reality, he was one of the sweetest people Ronny knew. Lefty would never hurt a fly; he didn't have to, one look at Lefty, and the fly would drop dead on the spot.

Lefty was happily married with three kids, but that didn't stop him from having a girlfriend on the side. His girlfriend was always seen chewing a big fat wad of gum. When they were together Lefty would hand her a stick of gum every five minutes to add to the already substantial amount she had in her mouth.

One day Ronny had to ask, "Lefty... what's with all the gum? Every five minutes you keep giving her another piece of gum. She looks like a damn chipmunk getting ready for winter. What's the deal?"

"When I was boxing they made me chew gum to strengthen my jaw. I've got her in training."

"What the hell are you talking about, training for what?"

"Blowjobs... she's conditioning her jaw muscles."

Lefty was a character. Ronny shared Lefty with another jockey, Will Nichols, a Louisiana mudbug. Together the three men would joke around in the jockey's room to the delight of the other jockeys. Ronny would accidentally-on-purpose kick a metal basin used for cleaning the floor so that it made the sound of a bell in a boxing match. This signaled Lefty to go into his act and feign a fight with Nichols. The jockeys would laugh and cheer as the two pretended to fight, the six-foot-five ex pugilist and the five-foot-two jockey.

Ronny would pretend to be the referee and get between the two men to break up the fight. Everyone in the room cheered and applauded. Ronny figured the act was too good to keep it isolated to the jockey's room so he suggested they take it on the road.

Instead of going to their regular watering hole, they'd find some place where nobody knew who they were. They'd sit and drink and run up a substantial bill and then they'd migrate to the bar where the cash register was situated. When the bartender pressed the key to open the cash register it set off the familiar bell sound that prompted Lefty and Nichols to go into their act.

Since the barkeeper didn't know it was an act, he worried the fight would start a riot causing a lot of damage. Ronny would offer to break up the fight and get his two friends out of the bar. The bartenders always quickly agreed. When Ronny asked about the substantial bill they'd rung up, the bartender usually said, "Forget it! Just get them the hell out of here."

Unfortunately things didn't turn out well for poor Lefty Fitzgerald. Ronny's mob collector friend Sal Latorre, worked with another fellow nicknamed Bats. Ronny never found out whether Bats was named for his penchant for solving collection problems with a baseball bat, or if it was because he was nuts as in, he had bats in his belfry.

In any case when Bats wasn't available, Sal would ask Lefty if he wanted to pick up a few bucks. All he had to do was stand behind Sal with his hand in his pocket and look scary. This was usually an effective collection technique.

Unfortunately Lefty's son was killed in a car accident and that seemed to push the ex fighter over the edge. After accompanying Sal on one of his collection runs he was picked up by the cops. All he had to do was keep his mouth shut. Nobody was going to testify against Sal, a known mob enforcer, or Lefty, his scary sidekick with a face not even a mother could love.

But instead of just keeping his mouth shut, the distraught ex fighter and jockey agent started talking and couldn't stop. He spouted so much gibberish that the cops figured he was off his rocker. Lefty Fitzgerald was sent to a hospital for the mentally ill. Meanwhile Ronny and Will Nichols had to leave Detroit for the next stop on the traveling circus known as professional thoroughbred racing

Rich, Cheap, And Stupid

In many ways the horse racing business is a reflection of society: you have the wealthy owners with their vested interests, and the working stiffs who keep the machinery of horse racing running as if they were indentured slaves held in place by financial need. Somewhere in the middle you have racing's middle class, the trainers and veterinarians. It's not surprising much of the racing establishment is found in the south. Times change, but somehow things stay remarkably the same.

After Ronny's racing days were over he got his trainer's license and started breaking horses for a fellow who had a stable of twenty-five thoroughbreds. Ronny's boss also owned the local racetrack. The son-of-a-bitch was as cheap as they come.

He wanted Ronny to train his horses and run the farm. He invited Ronny and his wife to his private Christmas party where he offered Ronny the job. Ronny said he would take the job for one hundred dollars a day plus ten percent of the earnings. The owner agreed and said he'd have his lawyer draw up a contract but Ronny said no.

"I don't want any written contract, especially one written by your lawyer. All I need is your word and a handshake." And Ronny stuck out his hand.

The owner stood there with his hands shoved so deep in his pockets he could almost touch his toes. The guy stood there staring at the ground. Ronny turned around, found his wife and left. The next day the owner showed up at the stables with a change of heart. But again he repeats the same legal mumbo jumbo, "I'll have my lawyer draw up a contract."

Ronny tells him, "Fuck your lawyer. All I need is your word. Now take your fat little hand out of your pocket and shake my hand or get lost."

The owner reluctantly takes his hand out of his pocket and shakes but Ronny won't let go. As he holds the owner's hand in a vice grip, he tells him, "You're giving me your word... you fuck me over and I'll make sure everyone in Ocala knows. You'll end up having to muck your own stables because no one will work for you. So be forewarned."

It's not just the jockeys that play fast and loose with the rules. Let's face it, if there's money involved, people will find a way to cheat, and it doesn't matter whether you're poor or rich, at the bottom of the ladder or at the top. If the authorities were serious about getting rid of the corruption and cheating, horse owners wouldn't be allowed to own tracks. It's an obvious conflict of interest.

One of the very first things the owner does once Ronny becomes the trainer is tell him to go to the Racing Secretaries Office and have him institute race conditions that are favorable to his horses. Conditions are the limits on what kind of horses can enter a particular race; for example, three-years old, non-winners of two races other than maidens, meaning: three-year old horses that have raced twice and lost both times.

A condition sets up a class of horses of equal experience, so the competition will appear to be fair.

What the track owner wanted was races that were specifically designed for his horses putting them in the best position to win. Unethical, but who was going to stop him. He owned the track, and if you wanted to keep your job, you did what you were told.

That wasn't the only advantage the track owner put in place for his horses. The owner had a horse called Lucky Luggage, a horse that should have long since retired, but this owner was going to push him until the bitter end. The horse was sore and didn't have a chance to win without some help from the pharmaceutical industry. Ronny knew what the horse needed in order to get him to the starting gate, but there was no way he was going to be the one to give it to him.

The owner called in a veterinarian and Ronny told him what the horse needed but the vet wanted no part of it. The owner told Ronny that the urine and blood taken from his winners never got to the state authorities, so Ronny told the vet. He reluctantly gave the horse what it needed to win, and it did. As promised by the owner, the state authorities had nothing to say.

What bothered Ronny the most about the owner was how cheap he was. Most of the staff that worked for Ronny lived hand-to-mouth. If they didn't get their paychecks at the end of the week, they wouldn't eat all weekend. Most of these people were married with children and they needed the money.

Every week the owner's son would arrive Friday afternoon with the paychecks for the staff but he always arrived after the banks had closed. In those days the banks closed early on Friday and weren't open again until Monday. The son-of-a-bitch owner did it on purpose so he could keep the payroll in the bank an extra couple of days, earning interest. The situation got so bad Ronny had to lend a number of his staff money just so they could eat over the weekend.

When Ronny confronted the owner about the situation, he admitted he did it to collect the extra interest. Ronny told him, "You pull that stunt again, and you can find yourself another trainer."

The following week the owner's son shows up after the banks had closed again, but this time Ronny had a plan. He takes the paychecks and his entire staff to the track's Information Window. Anyone who works at the track with an appropriate license, like Ronny, can cash checks at the Information Window. When the person behind the counter sees all the checks with the owners name on it he gets nervous. Ronny tells him to call the owner, and he'll speak to him.

When the owner gets on the line, Ronny tells him for the last time, "Cash the goddamn checks, or find another trainer."

The owner reluctantly cashes the checks. But some people just never learn. Of the twenty-five horses at the stable only two were any good, so Ronny suggested they should sell the rest and turn the money into a couple of good horses. Feeding and training a bunch of nags made no sense other than as a write-off for tax purposes.

Ronny proposes he take the horses, three at a time, to a track in New England where he thinks they might have a chance to win. If they do well in a few races, someone will be sure to make an offer to buy them. The owner agrees with the plan, so Ronny takes the first three horses up north.

The horses do well and sure enough someone wants to purchase all three for twenty-five hundred each. The owner says he'll fly up the following day to finalize the deal. The next day the owner arrives and speaks to the potential buyer. Ronny sees the buyer and asks if everything went as planned. The buyer says no. In addition to the twenty-five hundred per head, the owner demanded half the winnings from each horse's next winning purse. Ronny is livid. He had enough. He quits on the spot and flies back to Ocala. He had a new job running an even bigger farm within a week of his return.

I'm No Rat

That wasn't the only time a track owner or manager took advantage of their position in order to satisfy their own needs. Ronny was training a couple of his own horses at Latonia Park Racetrack in Kentucky. The manager approached Ronny and asked him if he could look after a pony for his son who liked to ride on the weekend. Technically, only racehorses were allowed in the stables but this was the man who ran the whole operation, and he was paying Ronny his regular day rate, so Ronny said yes. After a while the manager tells Ronny he wants him to look after a second pony for his wife who also liked to ride. So now Ronny is looking after his two racehorses and the manager's two ponies. The four horses take up four stalls.

The trainer in the next stall gets upset because he needs another stall and Ronny is taking up two spots that are supposed to be reserved for thoroughbreds. He bitches to Ronny, who suggests he keep his mouth shut, but the guy doesn't listen, and he complains to the office.

When the trainer who wants more stalls complains, he's told who owns the two ponies, and if he keeps yapping about it, he could find himself with no stalls at all. Every once in awhile you can beat the man, but in the long run, the man in charge almost always wins. Towing the line and rolling over for the powers that be, are two different things. Even Ronny has a line he won't cross.

One Saturday, this manager invites Ronny for lunch at a restaurant away from the track. The man, his son, and Ronny have a nice lunch. The man tells his son he has something to discuss with Ronny so he should wait in the car. After the boy leaves, the manager makes Ronny a proposition.

"I've noticed that you're not doing so well, so I thought I'd offer you an opportunity to make some extra money."

"I'm always interested in a little extra cash," says Ronny.

"We're having problems with the last race everyday. The favorites are always getting beat. Something is going on. Somebody is fixing these races."

"Well what's that got to do with me."

"I'll give you a special pass so you can go into the jockey's room. You know everybody and everybody likes you. You keep your eyes and ears open and report back to me as to what's going on. I'll make it worth your while."

"I'm sorry, I can't do that," Ronny says.

"Why not, I said I'd make it worth your while."

"Yeah, I heard you, but I just can't rat out these guys."

"Why not, what do you care?"

"I used to do the same thing. And I'm not going to squeal on my friends. I'm no rat. Thanks for lunch. Have a nice day." Ronny gets up and walks out.

The Vet and The Kerosene

Dr. Dubon's star pupil was a veterinarian by the name of Dr. Carlos Pedroza. He was rumored to have an I.Q. of one hundred and sixty. He was a weird little man who dressed like a hobo with wild frizzy hair that looked like he just stuck his finger in a light socket. Despite being a great horse doctor with lots of clients he was always short of money. Half the time he wouldn't take payment for his services, and when he did, he always undercharged.

The man was weird, but a genius when it came to horses. Ronny was breezing a horse for him when it took a tumble. Ronny told Pedroza what happened so the Doc could check him out.

Pedroza inspected the horse's leg, he then instructed Ronny to gallop the horse down the backstretch as he watched. Just by looking at how the horse galloped he correctly determined it had spread pasterns, something that can usually only be seen by taking an expensive series of x-rays. The man was one of the best veterinarians in the country.

Ronny met Pedroza during his riding days and the two men became tight. When Pedroza had a nice horse Ronny would be his jockey. Pedroza would climb up on the rail and watch as Ronny warmed up the horse before a race. If the horse was going well Ronny would signal Pedroza and he'd place a bet; if the horse was having an off day, he'd signal him not to bet. The two men worked well as a team.

Later on after Ronny stopped racing he would still go see Pedroza whenever he was in Kentucky. By this time Pedroza was getting up in age and his strength and eyesight weren't what they used to be. He asked Ronny if he could help around the farm he was renting. He should have been able to own his own farm but since he often forgot to get paid, he had to rent.

Pedroza got a call from a wealthy woman horse owner who had a fifteen-year old quality broodmare that couldn't throw a foal, meaning she could no longer give birth. She had spent thousands of dollars calling in every topnotch veterinarian in the country, but none of them could solve the problem.

She finally had enough and just wanted to get rid of the mare; at least she could get a tax write-off. She called Pedroza and told him the mare had been barren for three years; if he wanted her, he could have her. Pedroza examined the mare and decided to take her. The woman had the mare shipped to Pedroza's farm. When the horse arrived Pedroza called Ronny and told him he needed his help.

Because of Pedroza's failing eyesight, Ronny would drive him around and help assist in his examinations. Pedroza had Ronny drive to a gas station where he bought a gallon of kerosene.

"What are you going to do with that?" asked Ronny.

"You'll see," said Pedroza.

When they got back to the farm, Pedroza gets a twitch that he attaches to the horse's nose and upper lip. A twitch is just a stick with a loop of rope at one end. It's placed around the horse's nose and upper lip and twisted. The device is believed to calm the horse by releasing endorphins as pressure is applied. In theory it reduces stress and pain. Some regard it as ineffective voodoo nonsense, but sometimes these old methods actually work. Pedroza then gets his wife to hold the horse in the front while Ronny lifts the horse's tail and steadies her butt. Pedroza shoves a funnel into the horse's rear end. He pours a small amount of kerosene into her.

"What the hell are you doing," says Ronny," you're going to kill her."

"Nah, she'll be all right. This stuff will kill all the germs that are stopping her from conceiving." The horse expels all the kerosene.

"We do this two more times over the next week or so, and this bitch will being throwing foals like nobodies business."

And sure enough, after the treatment was completed, the mare was able to foal. She threw a nice little filly that could run. It ended up making one hundred and sixty thousand dollars. Two years later she threw another stake winner. The profits from the mare allowed Pedroza to buy his farm outright. Not bad for a freebie horse.

Sometimes the horse just won't co-operate.
Learn more in "The Fixer" - Rebel Seed Publishing

Part V

The Women

And So It Starts

While Ronny was in high school he was recruited at a pool hall to become a jockey. Ronny already had a run-in with the local cops that almost landed him in jail. His father warned him. If he got into trouble again, his parents would disown him. The opportunity to become a jockey was intriguing. The idea of big money and fame was tempting; it seemed like it was either become a jockey or descend into a life of petty crime. Little did he know there was very little difference.

He spent two years learning his trade from the ground up, literally from the ground up, mucking stalls and shoveling manure. When he reached the level of apprentice he felt it was time to treat himself to a new car, so he went downtown and bought himself a nice new Pontiac. To finalize the deal he had to go to the dealership office and sign some papers. When he got there the person he had to see was an attractive young woman who took an instant liking to the tough, rough-hewn bad-boy that walked in the door. The girl was the daughter of the wealthy dealership owner. The two started to date and the relationship quickly got serious on the young girl's side. Ronny on the other hand was oblivious to the significance of the young ladies desire.

The girl's parents were snooty, Anglo-Saxon Rosedale types, Rosedale being a wealthy part of town where the inhabitants were bankers, lawyers, and wealthy business magnets. They were refined genteel people who were members of the best clubs: places that served the finest cuisine, twelve-year old rye whiskey, and had absolutely no Jewish members, or anyone that couldn't trace their heritage back to the Magna Carta.

Despite the cultural divide the parents indulged their daughter's infatuation with the heathen Hebrew, and invited Ronny to dinner. When Ronny arrived he was ushered into a dining room that was bigger than his parent's entire house. The table, chairs, and walls were cover in expensive dark stained walnut. The paintings on the walls featured English gentlemen in their bright red hunting garb surrounded by dogs all eager for the thrill of the hunt. The placed smelled like money.

When the butler poured Ronny a glass of wine and waited for approval, Ronny didn't know what to do. He stuck his hand in his pocket and pulled out a five-dollar bill to tip him; but his young lady stopped him whispering, "Just tell him it's okay."

Ronny downs the entire glass in one long gulp, looks at the stuff-shirt penguin and says, "Yeah, it'll do."

If ever there was a fish out of water, Ronny was it. Despite the clash of class, the two sweethearts were happy. To the young lady's parents' credit, their main concern was their daughter's happiness. If she chose this young man from the wrong side of the tracks, and if he made her happy, so be it. And then it happened.

Ronny was just an apprentice and despite the potential he had shown he was still inexperienced. The owner of the stable wanted to teach the brash young upstart a lesson so he put Ronny on a horse that only an experienced jockey should have ridden. Ronny couldn't control the animal and despite winning the race, he wiped out most of the field in the process.

The stewards suspended him for the rest of the meet. Ronny needed to race to gain experience, so his contract was loaned out to an owner in Quebec. Ronny told his girl that he had to go to Montreal. She was distraught. She demanded to go with him but Ronny told her it was impossible. Apprentice jockeys live in tack rooms at the track, and it was unrealistic for her to come and live with him. The situation got increasingly tense. Then Ronny got a phone call from the girl's father telling him his daughter tried to commit suicide. She was in the hospital and could he please come and talk to her.

Ronny's mother warned him, "What kind of crazy *shiksa* have you got involved with. Stay away from her, she's trouble."

But Ronny went to see her. Her father said he would pay for the girl to go to Montreal where she could see Ronny whenever he wasn't riding. Ronny didn't know what else to do so he agreed. Ronny liked the girl, but he was just starting his career, and the last thing he needed was an unstable woman to look after.

He was young, and still had more than his share of wild oats to sow. After a while, a wealthy woman horse owner from

Kentucky bought Ronny's contract and took him down to her farm in Kentucky. That put an end to Ronny's first serious and almost fatal relationship with a woman.

Annie Get Your Son

A few years later Ronny was back in Montreal with the car dealer's daughter a distant memory. An attractive young blonde, Annie, started coming around the track spending time with her father who was a trainer. Ronny and Annie met and started to date. Before too long the relationship got serious and Ronny proposed marriage. Despite both being racehorse people, Annie's father wasn't pleased.

Annie and her family were French Canadian Catholics while Ronny was an Anglo Jew from hated Toronto. Despite their differences the two young lovers were determined to tie the knot. Annie wanted to get married in a church by a priest and Ronny was prepared to go along despite the fact it disappointed his Holocaust-surviving father and mother.

In order to get married in a church by a priest they had to ask permission. The priest presented Ronny with a series of demands including raising the children Catholic and forking over an annual percentage of his earnings. Ronny refused, and so the two young lovers headed across the border to Cornwall, Ontario where they got married by a justice of the peace.

Life with Annie was interesting. Despite Ronny's wild and often threatening lifestyle Annie was determined to make the marriage work. They got along well with few arguments or problems other than the seemingly endless sticky situations Ronny found himself in. In truth, Annie was attracted to the bad boy in Ronny's nature. They had three children, two boys and a girl. As the kids grew into teenagers it became clear the oldest boy was becoming a problem. Despite the fact he could have become a world-class jockey under Ronny's guidance, the boy preferred a life of petty thievery. Ronny was getting fed-up with the kid's behavior and worried that the boy's run-ins with the law would eventually slop over onto him. That was something he was not prepared to live with.

Ronny and Annie had a farm in Ocala, Florida where Ronny made a living buying and selling horses. On the weekend he would scout around for animals that didn't sell at auction, looking for that diamond in the rough. Occasionally good horses get passed up because of superficial reasons like a scar from running into a fence, something that has nothing to do with the horse's ability to run.

Because the banks were closed on the weekend, Ronny kept a stash of five thousand dollars in a strongbox in the house, just in case he wanted to make a quick deal. At the time he actually had fifty-two hundred in the box. Ronny wasn't worried about leaving that kind of money in the house. He was the only one with a key to the strongbox and he had two large pit bulls that were on constant guard.

On one of his weekend scouting missions he found a horse he liked, and made a deal with the owner. He told the owner he'd go home and get the money and be right back to finalize the sale. When he got home to get the money he found the strongbox had been pried open and all the money was missing.

Ronny knew exactly who took it and he told Annie. "Your son stole fifty-two hundred dollars from us." Annie, always protective of the boy, didn't believe it.

"It had to be him, nobody but the family knew about the money; the other kids would never do anything like that. It had to be somebody the dogs knew, or they would have ripped whoever it was apart. And besides, the little shit didn't come home last night. He's afraid I'll kill him, and maybe that's exactly what I'm going to do."

Ronny heads out to the truck to find the boy with Annie tagging along, just to make sure Ronny doesn't follow through on his threat. They visit several of their son's friends, but none of them know, or would admit that they knew where he was.

When they finally got home there's a message from Ronny's friend, Moreno, the Cuban drug dealer who owned a restaurant in town where Ronny's son occasionally worked. The boy and his friend were at his house. They must have figured the Cuban would protect them. Ronny and Annie get back in the truck and go right over. When they get there the two boys are on their knees in the middle of Moreno's living room crying their eyes out, begging the Cuban to protect them. When Ronny enters the house, it takes all his will power to not kick his son in the head.

Annie begs Ronny to hold his temper and forgive the boy. The kid is crying. He blames the other kid who in turn blames him. Ronny is ready to kill him but Annie throws herself in front of the boy begging Ronny to let it go. Ronny looks at his wife with fire in his eyes.

"The little shit took everything, he didn't even leave us two hundred bucks to buy food. Annie... the kid's no-good, you don't want me to hurt him, fine. I'm calling the cops."

The kid is crying. Annie's begging. And Ronny's fuming. He picks up the phone but Moreno stops him. "Ronny, my friend, none of us need the cops."

Ronny puts down the phone and looks at his son. "From this moment on you don't have a father. We're done. I don't want to see you, hear you, or know anything about you. If I see you anywhere near the house, I'll kill you."

Ronny walks out and goes home. When Annie and Ronny get home Annie begs Ronny to change his mind but Ronny is adamant. She tells Ronny the boy only has two weeks before graduation, could he please let him stay until then? Ronny relents but tells Annie he's moving to Moreno's until the boy graduates. After graduation Ronny comes home and Annie starts again, begging Ronny to forgive the boy. Ronny says no. He takes the boys belongings, throws them out on the front lawn, and lights a match to them. He tells Annie the boy better never show his face around the house again.

The household gets increasingly tense with Annie constantly demanding Ronny let the boy return, but Ronny sticks to his guns. He won't have anything to do with the kid. The situation remains the same until the day of Ronny's birthday. He arrives home from the track. When he walks into the house, Annie and his oldest son are standing there holding hands. They shout, "Happy birthday!"

That's the last straw. Ronny remains outwardly calm although he's seething on the inside. "I told you, it was either him or me. Make your choice."

"He's my son," says Annie, "and he'll always be my son, no matter what he does."

Ronny goes into the bedroom, packs some clothes, hands Annie the keys to the farm and says, "The kid and the farm are yours. I'm just taking the truck."

He walks out, gets into the truck, and starts to drive off. He gets about fifty yards down the road when he hears Annie shouting. She's running after him. Ronny stops and waits for her.

When she gets to the truck, she asks, "When are you coming home?"

"Never," he says flatly. "We're done. You made your choice. It's over."

A few bottles of cheap wine does the trick.
Learn more in "The Fixer" - Rebel Seed Publishing

Unlucky In Love

After his divorce from Annie, Ronny moves to Detroit to stay with his Armenian friend, Vartan. They own a couple of horses together and Vartan lends Ronny some money to get his cosmetic business off the ground. Vartan introduces Ronny to his cousin, a beautiful and wealthy woman that he has been trying unsuccessfully to fix up for years. Everyone he introduces is rejected, but when she meets Ronny there's an instant attraction. The two fall in love and she asks Ronny if he's interested in getting married. He tells her he would, but he's promised his parents that if he ever got married again, the woman would have to be Jewish, or she'd have to convert. The woman, whose name is Virginia, says she would consider it.

Virginia develops trouble with her teeth. It requires a root canal. She's terrified of doctors but decides she must get it done. Despite having a gum infection, the dentist proceeds with the root canal, a disastrous decision that ends up causing the infection to run rampant throughout her body, damaging her kidneys forcing her to go on dialysis.

She needed a new kidney and is lucky enough to have a cousin who is a match and is willing to be a donor. On the day of the surgery she drives to the hospital, but when she gets there she keeps on driving, fearful the operation will go wrong. She cannot come to grips with the necessity of the surgery, no matter what Ronny says to her. Without the operation she will die. She manages to hang on for three years, but ultimately the damage is too great and she passes on. The second woman Ronny really loved is now gone.

While spending the winter in Louisiana, Ronny meets another nice woman that he falls in love with. She's a beautician who offers to help him develop the fragrance for his beauty cream. They work together closely to resolve the fragrance issue that finalizes the development of the product. The woman is not without her share of problems: she has MS, two children, and she's married to a multimillionaire bigamist who is never there.

Her husband splits his time between his three wives who initially didn't know about each other, but having three wives is not the kind of thing you can keep a secret for long. The millionaire philanderer in question keeps the women quiet by sending each of them three thousand dollars a month. Ronny's new girlfriend finds herself in a tough spot; she's sick with an expensive, incurable, debilitating disease. She depends on her bigamist husband to help pay her medical expenses. The disease progresses to a point where her husband and son decide to place her in an out-of-state sanatorium.

The husband knows about Ronny and his relationship with his wife. He asks Ronny what it would take for him to take his wife off his hands. Ronny tells the bigamist millionaire that he loves the woman and would take care of her. He doesn't want a cent for himself, but in order to look after her properly, the husband would have to give his wife one million dollars for medical expenses. The bigamist says he'll think about it and call Ronny back. He never does.

Ronny stays in touch with the woman but because she has basically given her husband and her son Power of Attorney, there is little he can do. He sees her whenever he can, and calls her every week until one day there is no answer. The woman has passed away. The loss of these women affected Ronny deeply.

And then there were the women that were just plain trouble.

Crazy Bitches Part One

Ronny was riding for trainer Dwayne Hickok, a six-foot four-inch tall drink of water. Looking at the two of them discussing a mount was like watching a live action version of the old *Mutt and Jeff* comic strip that used to be in *the funny papers*. Hickok had a crazy filly called Miss Susaki, and this bitch was nuts. Any time a jockey tried to mount her she would flip. She was so hard to handle she had to be loaded in the starting gate last, or else she would cause mayhem. As soon as the gate closed behind her the starter would start the race in order to avoid any accidents. The bitch may have been nuts but boy could she run. As soon as the gate opened she would take off as if someone shoved a rocket up her ass. The only jockey around that could handle her was Ronny, and with him in the saddle, the filly was a consistent winner.

Ronny and Miss Susaki made a good team. His relationship with the filly was as good as any relationship he had with any female of any species. In fact the horse and jockey had done so well Hickok decided to enter her in a major Stake Race, The Dominion Mile, but instead of giving Ronny the mount, Hickok brings in world famous jockey Willie Wannamaker. Ronny was hot. He took it as a personal insult, and it was. He asked Hickok why he gave Wannamaker the mount.

"Why did you bring in Wannamaker? You know that bitch is crazy. What the hell's the matter with you? You want him to get killed?"

But Hickok held his ground. "Look Ronny, it's not me, it's the owners. They want Wannamaker, and that's that."

Ronny wasn't happy, "You're a fucking idiot, you big son-of-a-bitch!" Ronny tries to kick him in the knee, but he's too short for the lanky cowboy and gets him in the shin. "I quit!"

Ronny was fed up and out of a job. He figured he needed to calm down, and the best way to do that was to take a vacation. Every week he would have his paycheck automatically deposited in the bank across from the track. He figured he must have squirreled away at least three thousand bucks by now, just enough to find some action, get drunk, and have some fun.

Ronny cleaned himself up, and changed into his street clothes including his well-worn favorite tweed jacket with the slight rip in the lining. He had enough of the bullshit, and deserved a little R-and-R. He went across the street to the bank and asked for the manager. He told the bank manager he wanted to closeout his account.

"All right Mr. Kleinberg, we'll look after that right away. It's a substantial sum so I'll have a guard escort you back to your car."

"A guard? I don't need a guard for three thousand bucks."

"Mr. Kleinberg, it's thirty thousand dollars, not three thousand."

"You got to be shitting me?"

"I'm a bank manager Mr. Kleinberg, we don't shit."

When they brought in the thirty thousand dollars cash, Ronny didn't know what to do with it. The bank manager offered a bag but Ronny declined.

"Nah, I'll just shove it in my jacket." So Ronny proceeded to rip a bigger whole in the lining of his favorite tweed jacket while he shoved stacks of hundred dollar bills in the lining. For the next few weeks, Ronny hardly took the jacket off. He even slept with it on.

As he leaves the bank he notices a travel agency with a big sign offering special discounts on Mediterranean Cruises. He crosses the street and goes in. He books a European vacation, a flight to New York, and an overnight stay at the Waldorf Astoria. He wants to make sure he's fresh and raring to go for his European adventure.

Before he leaves the travel agency he tips the pretty agent a hundred bucks. He then sends his mother in Toronto a few thousand dollars. The travel agent booked him into a deluxe suite at the Waldorf but when he got into his room all he saw was a bed, a desk, and a big fancy cabinet, no television. Ronny got angry. He called down to the front desk to complain, demanding that for the money he was paying they could provide a damn TV. The patient desk clerk explained that the television was in the cabinet. Ronny still had a lot to learn about traveling first class.

Three months later Ronny returned to Louisville broke, but happy. All that was left of the thirty thousand dollars was thirty-six bucks, but it was one hell of a vacation.

Crazy Bitch Part Two

Ronny was relaxed and ready to get back to work, so he called Dwayne Hickok figuring his shin had heeled by now.
Ronny was still one of the best riders around so Hickok quickly agreed to take him back, and he got some mounts immediately.

Ronny noticed that a great looking young blonde had started coming around to visit Hickok, it turned out to be Hickok's daughter. A pretty blonde was like catnip to Ronny, but before he could make his move, Hickok gathered all his staff and made an announcement.

"I don't want any of you assholes sniffing around my daughter. Don't talk to her, don't look at her, and don't think about her, and that means you, Kleinberg! Keep away if you know what's good for you."

Ronny was interested in the girl, but with only thirty-six bucks in his pocket, he figured he didn't have a shot. He had no choice but to obey Hickok's announcement. He needed the job.

Fast-forward thirty years; Ronny is now a trainer and divorced. He signs up for one of those dating groups where everybody fills in a card with their background details. The participants look through the cards hoping to find a compatible match. It's an old fashion analog version of today's numerous dating websites. If someone in the group is interested in one of the cards, they call to set up a date for coffee, or whatever. In Ronny's case he was more interested in the whatever.

Ronny can spot a winning horse from a hundred yards away while driving in his car, but women aren't horses. You can't tell the crazy ones just by looking. And you can't walk up to one, and feel if their hip is in proper alignment to their hock to ascertain if they can perform.

Ronny got a call from a woman who was part of the dating group. She noticed he was in the horse racing business. It was something they had in common. Her name was Sandra.

She was a lawyer that was being groomed to become the State Attorney General. What she didn't tell Ronny was the pressure of the job had got to her, and she started to drink heavily.

Drinking has never been known as the best way to enhance a career, especially if you're a mean drunk; and as you will learn, when this woman drank, she became one scary bitch. In any case their initial conversation went well and they arranged a date. When she walked into the coffee shop Ronny recognized her immediately, it was Hickok's daughter. Despite the thirty years she was still one good-looking woman. Ronny and Sandra started a relationship.

One night they were out for dinner and she starts to drink. The more she drank the more argumentative she became. Whatever Ronny said it was wrong or stupid. The more she drank the worse she got. Ronny figured some fresh air and a drive might sober her up and calm her down. So they finish their meal and Ronny suggests they go for a drive. As they're driving she starts again, and no matter what Ronny says it's the stupidest thing she's ever heard. Finally Ronny's had enough.

"Okay Sandra, enough is enough. If you don't shut the fuck up right now, I'm going to stop the car, and you can get out and walk home."

Well as you might expect this did not go over well. "You asshole, I'll have you know I was almost the State's Attorney General. I'm a respected lawyer and you can't talk to me like that."

That was the last straw. Ronny pulls the car over to the side of the road at the top of a steep hill. "You could've been the State's Attorney General if you weren't such a fucking scary bitch when you drink. Now get the hell out of my car. You can walk home"

"Are you nuts? It's three miles and I'm wearing high heels!"

"Serves you right. You're acting like one crazy bitch. Now get out!"

"I will not!"

"We'll see about that." Ronny gets out of the car and goes around to the passenger side. He opens the door and grabs her.

She's holding onto the seat like it's a life preserver, but Ronny eventually manages to get her out. As he drives off he feels bad, it's cold, she's dressed in a short skimpy outfit, and she's wearing high heels. And yes it's at least three miles to her house.

He slows the car down so he can turn around and pick her up. Maybe the cool air has sobered her up and calmed her down. He looks in the rear view mirror. He sees her defiantly standing at the top of the hill on her wobbly high heels with one hand on her hip and the other raised in the air giving him the finger.

"That's one crazy bitch!" Ronny keeps on driving leaving her standing there. You may think that's the end of the story, but its not. Like they say in the infomercials 'but wait, there's more.'

You Gotta Know The Password

Ronny was staying with a friend Dewey Smith. For the next week Sandra keeps calling repeatedly trying to apologize. She desperately wants to see Ronny but he won't answer the phone or return her calls. Dewey is intrigued by the stories and the phone calls. He wants to meet her and see what she looks like, but Ronny is having none of it.

"Listen Dewey she's crazy. I don't want anything to do with her."

"You're exaggerating, she can't be as bad as you say."

"She's nuts. I'll tell you how nuts she is. She has three Lincoln Continentals."

"Yeah, so she's rich."

"You know why she has three Lincoln Continentals?"

"No. Why?"

"Cause when one runs out of gas, she uses the next one until it runs out of gas. She's a nut case, and don't ever get in her way when she starts to drink."

Just then there's a knock on the door. Ronny looks out the peephole. It's Sandra wearing her fur coat. Ronny turns to Dewey.

"You want to see what she looks like, take a look." So Dewey looks through the peephole. "She's nice looking."

The knocking continues none stop. "I know you're in there Ronny. I've got to see you. Open up. Please!"

Ronny looks through the peephole figuring he'll have some fun with her. "You want to come in, you've got to give me the secret password." Dewy is standing behind Ronny chuckling.

"What secret password, what are you talking about?"

"You can't come in unless you know the secret password." Sandra flings open her fur coat, arms stretched out as far as they can go. She's stark naked.

"That's the secret password!" says Ronny, and he opens the door. Dewey stares at Sandra who has dropped her fur coat. She's standing there without a stitch of clothes on.

Ronny turns to Dewy, "Well you did want to see her. There she is, that's all of her!"

Sal and Bats had their various collection techniques.
Learn more in "The Fixer" - Rebel Seed Publishing

You Don't Have To Be Married To Be Screwed

After Ronny retired from riding he started a business breaking racehorses in Ocala, Florida. Breaking horses is the process of getting young horses accustomed to carrying a rider, and preparing them for a future in horse racing.

A Mrs. Rotman came to see him. She owned a couple of broodmares; broodmares are female thoroughbreds that are used for breeding. She had a couple of horses from these broodmares that she wanted broken. Ronny tells her his price, which at the time was twenty-five dollars a day. He starts breaking the horses as arranged per their agreement. She comes by every month to pay. There's never any problem or incident.

On one such visit she tells Ronny she has a filly in Miami that she is having delivered to him. When it arrives she wants to discuss a new agreement. The woman wants to save the expense of getting the horse ready to race, so she proposes a fifty-fifty arrangement in lieu of paying the cost of breaking.

When the horse arrives Ronny takes one look at it and sees the horse has a condition called *osselets*: a bony growth on the fetlock or ankle joint resulting in inflammation of the enveloping membrane. In this case it was green; a sign that the condition was in the early stages, characterized by hot, soft swelling.

Osselets is caused by concussion and strain on the fetlock, usually on the front legs. Without treatment and rest the condition can become chronic. This horse required an extended period of rest, plus a treatment called *pin firing*, done by a licensed veterinarian. Today the condition would be treated with rest plus ointment, rather than the outdated *thermocautery* pin firing method. The cost of caring for the horse while it rested, the veterinarian treatments, and the cost of readying the horse for racing made the deal uneconomical.

Obviously the woman was looking for something-for-nothing. Ronny wasn't interested in the deal. Mrs. Rotman decided she didn't want to invest any more money on the horse. She preferred to give it away to avoid the expense of an extended period of treatment, plus the cost of breaking. She offered the horse to Ronny for nothing, in order to avoid the necessary expenses.

Ronny had already checked out the horse's track record and found that it finished poorly in both its previous outings. He didn't want the horse, even for nothing; but he thinks about it and ultimately decides to accept the deal. Maybe after some rest and treatment he can turn the horse into some money. Mrs. Rotman signs over the title.

Ronny calls in a veterinarian who treats the horse and recommends three months rest with no training or strenuous activity. After three months of expense the horse has recovered and Ronny starts the training process. When the horse is ready, Ronny enters her in a series of races. Each time she races she finishes better. Finally in her fourth race she wins but the time is slow.

While in the winner's circle someone in the crowd shouts out to Ronny and asks if he's willing to sell the horse. Ronny tells the fellow he's prepared to let her go for thirty-five hundred dollars, the same amount he received as the winning purse. Ronny tells the man to meet him at the Spit Barn with the money. The Spit Barn is where the winning horse is taken for urine and if necessary blood collection. The sample is sent off to a lab for testing to make sure the horse didn't have any illegal substances in its system. The buyer arrives with the money and Ronny signs over the ownership papers for the horse.

A few days later, there's a knock on Ronny's door. It's the Sheriff. He hands Ronny a summons ordering him to court in the matter of the ownership of the horse he just sold. Ronny isn't concerned because he has a photocopy of the dated title that Mrs. Rotman signed when she turned the horse over to him.

When they arrive in court Mrs. Rotman shows up with a lawyer claiming she is the actual owner of the horse. She is demanding the thirty-five hundred dollars from the winning purse, plus the thirty-five hundred Ronny received for selling the horse.

Ronny explains the circumstances of his acquiring the horse. He details the expenses he incurred in treating the horse's injuries as well as the costs associated with preparing the horse to race. He also shows the judge the photocopy of the title Mrs. Rotman signed when she turned the horse over to him. The Judge believes Ronny's story but tells him that his photocopy of the signed title is not sufficient evidence to prove ownership. According to Florida law, a signed and dated bill of sale stating that the horse is being sold, and in what condition the horse is in at the time of sale is required.

The Judge acknowledges the expense Ronny has incurred in treating and caring for the horse, so he decides to split the proceeds, awarding Mrs. Rotman thirty-five hundred dollars. Ronny was screwed. The nice Mrs. Rotman turned out to be a conniving con artist. Ronny never had much luck with women both personally or in business.

Eventually You Learn Your Lesson

A few years later Ronny was managing a large farm as well as evaluating and buying horses for the owner. The owner was interested in a horse that was owned by a woman in Pennsylvania. Ronny was told to go and negotiate a deal with the woman to acquire the horse that was worth a hundred thousand dollars. It's common practice for someone who acts as an agent in the acquisition of a thoroughbred to receive a commission on the sale.

Ronny went to Pennsylvania and negotiated the hundred thousand dollar sale as well as a ten percent commission for himself. He had the woman owner sign and date a piece of paper saying she will pay Ronny a ten per cent commission on the sale price of the horse for acting as the agent. The deal is consummated and three weeks later Ronny receives a check for five thousand dollars, not ten.

Ronny complains to the woman but she says five percent is enough and that's all she's paying. Ronny has no choice but to take the matter to court. In court the Judge asks Ronny if he is a licensed agent, to which Ronny explains he doesn't have to be licensed. He negotiated the sale making him the de facto agent and therefore is entitled to a commission to which the woman agreed.

The woman argues that even the top thoroughbred agents like Taylor Made only get five percent, but Ronny counters that the sales company also receives five percent, for a total commission of ten percent. Since he acted alone cutting out the middleman, he therefore is entitled to the full ten per cent. He produces the dated piece of paper the woman signed agreeing to the ten percent commission. The Judge looks at the paper and asks the woman if she signed it. The woman is a bit flustered.

"That's not an official document, it's just a scrap of paper."

The Judge looks at the woman, "It doesn't matter if the agreement is written on a piece of toilet paper as long as it has the required information. This document appears to be valid. It says you owe Mr. Kleinberg a ten percent commission on the sale of the said horse that was sold for one hundred thousand dollars. It is dated, and signed by what appears to be your signature. Do you remember signing this piece of paper?"

"Ah... well... I really don't remember."

The Judge is not amused by the woman's obvious obfuscation. "Show me your driver's license?" The woman hesitates fumbling in her purse as if she can't find it.

The Judge is getting annoyed. "Show me your driver's license now or I'll charge you with contempt."

The woman finally retrieves her license and hands it to the Judge. The Judge holds up Ronny's piece of paper along with the woman's driver's license in order to compare the signatures.

"Are you trying to tell me this is not your signature? And let me remind you, perjury is a jailable offense."

The woman reluctantly acknowledges her signature and Ronny is awarded the additional five thousand dollars. Ronny was not going to let this woman pull the same stunt as Mrs. Rotman. You can cheat Ronny once but you'll never get away with it again.

The Contest

During the winter Ronny usually spent his time in Florida, but in the spring and summer he would make his way to Detroit where he had a number of close friends. While in Detroit he'd meet up with his pals Sal Latorre, the mob enforcer who moonlighted as head of the pari-mutuel windows at the track, and an Armenian businessman Vartan Saroyan. The three men would either hang out at The Pig Farm Saloon or The Blow-Out Nightclub. Tonight The Blow Out was the watering hole of choice. It was a place frequented by gamblers, mobsters, and racetrack cronies.

The three men sat in the back surveying the new crop of skimpily clad cocktail waitresses that were the place's main attraction. A new girl had started and she was a knockout. A number of the Blow Out regulars had tried to date her, and I use the term date loosely, but none had been successful. As usual, Ronny had a plan to break the ice.

"I know how we can all get to her."

"Bullshit," says the Armenian, "I've talked to at least five guys that approached her, and they all got turned down. One guy got a fat lip for his trouble."

"Don't worry about it, just watch me." Ronny gets up from the table and goes over to the young waitress who is standing at the bar. Ronny's friends are laughing, wondering if Ronny will be the next victim of the woman's left hook. They watch as Ronny approaches the attractive waitress. She's wearing a skintight faux leather black dress that barely extends to her hips. Its neckline plunges to a point just below her navel. She stands about five foot eight but in her six-inch backless patent leather stilettos she takes on Amazon proportions.

If Ronny stood any closer he could almost rest his chin on the ledge created by her substantial cleavage: two soft billows of pulchritude that teasingly wanted a way out of their faux leather bondage. The men watch in amazement as the beauty and the beast discuss terms.

When Ronny gets back to the table Sal asks, "So what did she say?"

"She said she'd think about it."

"But what did you tell her?" asks Vartan.

"I told her we were operating a Florida Winter Contest."

Sal looks at Ronny like he's nuts, "What the hell is a Florida Winter Contest?"

"I told her we were organizing a contest for an all expense paid winter in Florida; open to a select few attractive women. Each woman would be scored on a scale of one to ten, and the woman that had the highest score would win. The winner can stay at my friend's place in Tampa, he's never there, and he gave me the keys."

"Yah but what do they have to do to get a score?" asks Vartan.

"What do you think dummy? They have to screw the three of us. We're the judges."

The whole thing was a drunken joke but within a few days Ronny was getting calls from the other waitresses at the bar wanting to know if they could get in on the contest. By the time the original girl called to confirm her entrance, Ronny had five other beautiful waitresses on the list. Sal had a trailer out by the lake where no one would bother them. Ronny prepared a schedule and taped it to the trailer wall. Each judge rated each contestant. Their scores were posted on the schedule.

The original reluctant contestant ended up having a voracious appetite and refused to accept her initial score. She demanded a do-over. Ronny happily agreed and posted a perfect ten, after which she announced. "Okay, now we're talking… call the other guys to come over… Florida here I come!"

What goes on behind the scenes in horse racing.
Learn more in "The Fixer" - Rebel Seed Publishing

Part VI

More Than Just Horses

Doctor Death and The Picture

Ronny's friend Vartan owned a small greasy spoon in Royal Oak, Michigan. They were close. They were partners in a couple of horses, and Vartan later helped Ronny establish his beauty cream business. Vartan was a distant cousin to Doctor Jack Kevorkian, best known for his championing terminal patients' right to die, a procedure known as physician-assisted suicide. Kevorkian is said to have helped one hundred and thirty people end their lives.

Kevorkian was not just a medical activist: he was a pathologist, painter, author, composer, and instrumentalist. He never married, spoke eight languages, and was in constant conflict with the authorities over his right-to-die activities.

Every morning Jack Kevorkian went to Vartan's restaurant for breakfast where he'd met Ronny. Ronny and Kevorkian became good friends over the breakfast special. The three men would also play a weekly, Friday night poker game at the antique shop down the street. One evening while playing cards Ronny noticed that Kevorkian looked down in the dumps. He asked what was bothering him.

"Somebody broke into my apartment."

"Did they take anything?" Ronny asks.

"No, nothing was taken."

"Did you call the cops?"

"Sure I called the cops."

"What did they say?"

'Nothing... they said there wasn't anything they could do."

'Figures," says Ronny, "that's because it was the cops."

"What are you talking about?"

Ronny explains his theory that it was the police that broke into his apartment looking for something to hang on him. The cops and the government were determined to get Kevorkian. He was tried four times between 1994 and 1997. He was acquitted the first three times with the fourth time a mistrial. They finally got Kevorkian after he allowed the CBS News program *60 Minutes* to air a video of him participating in the voluntary euthanasia of a patient in the final stages of Lou Gehrig's disease. He was convicted of second-degree homicide and sentenced to ten to twenty-five years in prison. He served eight years finally being released, but only after he was diagnosed with a terminal illness.

Ronny remembers having breakfast with Kevorkian at Vartan's restaurant. Sitting at the end of the counter were four older women who overheard the conversation between Ronny and Kevorkian regarding physician-assisted suicide. One of the women who was wearing a large gold cross approached Kevorkian and got up in his face.

"Who made you God?" she says.

Kevorkian reaches into his pocket and pulls out an old tattered photograph of an elderly woman strapped to a wheel chair. Kevorkian hands the woman the picture and explains she was in constant pain; she had an incurable disease. He goes on to tell her that the woman's daughter came to him, begging him to help end her mother's suffering.

He let the woman look at the photograph carefully for a moment. "Unless you have a relative in a similar condition as this poor woman, you have no business discussing this problem with me."

He takes the photo from the woman's hand, sticks it back in the breast pocket of his jacket, and turns back to his breakfast special.

The Kentucky Standoff

In Kentucky minor incidents have a history of turning into long running feuds, the most famous being the feud between the Hatfield's of Kentucky and the McCoy's of West Virginia. Despite numerous skirmishes, slights, and even murders involving members of the two families nothing of historic consequence resulted, that is, until the ultimate insult was inflicted.

When Asa Harmon McCoy was murdered, most likely by Devil Anse Hatfield for being a Union sympathizer during the Civil War, no feud erupted. When Devil Anse Hatfield used his political clout to win a land dispute with a McCoy cousin, Perry Cline, involving a five thousand acre plot of land, no feud resulted; but when Randle McCoy accused Floyd Hatfield of stealing his pig, all hell broke loose, leading to a thirty year war. In Kentucky there is no dispute too small that someone won't try and solve it with a gun.

Ronny was training some horses for a lawyer while living in Kentucky with his wife and kids. It was cold, the track was frozen, and things were just plain bad. Because the conditions were so bad, the races were cancelled. When races are cancelled nobody works and things come to a virtual standstill.

Ronny was renting a house on a hill over-looking a stream. Ronny's landlord was an old-timer who owned the local general store located just across the river below Ronny's rented house. The landlord had a Chow. Chows are not known for their love of strangers, and this Chow was no exception. The dog had bitten several people in the past, but that didn't stop its hillbilly owner from letting the beast run free.

It had just snowed so Ronny's wife, Annie, took the kids outside to play with their new toboggan. The landlord's Chow was running loose and saw Annie and the kids playing. The dog either thought Annie was hurting the kids, or maybe it just wanted to join in on the fun. The end result was the dog bites Annie on the leg causing a bad case of phlebitis. Ronny takes Annie to the doctor who immediately sends her to the hospital.

Ronny is stuck around the house looking after the kids, taking them to school, and picking them up. When he can, he goes to the track to look after the horses he's training. After about two weeks Ronny realizes the hospital bills are adding up and he doesn't have insurance so he goes over to the landlord's store and asks to talk to the owner. Since it was the landlord's dog that bit Ronny's wife, he asks him if he could help with the medical expenses.

The landlord throws Ronny out of his store. "Get the hell out of my store, and don't come back!"

It's not the response Ronny hoped for or expected. He speaks to the lawyer who owns the horses he's training. The lawyer says not to worry. He'll handle it. Ronny dictates his statement to the lawyer's secretary and the lawyer tells Ronny to make sure he pays the rent. When Ronny goes to pay the rent, the landlord won't take it. He demands Ronny and his family get out of his house immediately.

Ronny contacts the lawyer again and tells him what happened. The lawyer tells Ronny to drop off the checks for the rent to him; he tells Ronny that there is a law in Kentucky that says you can't evict someone with children until the school year is over. Since it's February and the school year ends in June, the landlord can't evict him.

The landlord serves Ronny with an Eviction Notice anyway. Ronny and his lawyer take the hillbilly to court. Both sides explain their stories, and the Judge informs the landlord that he cannot evict Ronny and his family from the house until the school year is finished.

The landlord objects but the Judge is firm. He even issues a Restraining Order on the landlord barring him from coming within a hundred yards of the house. If that wasn't enough, the landlord had to pay all of Annie's medical expenses because the dog had a history of biting people. And since his insurance company refused to pay, the landlord had to pay everything out of his own pocket.

The next day Ronny hears what sounds like gunshots outside his house. He goes to the picture window at the front of the house that overlooks the river. He sees the crazy old hillbilly firing a pistol at the rocks on the edge of the stream. Ronny is standing there watching the old fart when a bullet whistles through the window missing Ronny's head by a foot or so. It embeds itself in the wall of the living room where his children play. Ronny goes to the closet and gets his shotgun. He marches out of the house and down to the riverbank. He raises his shotgun and aims it directly at the hillbilly landlord.

"Hay asshole, you fire one more fucking shot, and I'll drop you where you stand. My wife and kids are in that house. Are you completely nuts?"

The old man puts down the gun and runs back to his store. Ronny goes back to his house seething mad. About an hour later Ronny is sitting in his living room when he notices a series of heads popping up in front of his window. He gets up and goes to look. A heavily armed police swat team surrounds the house. Ronny yells to the cops that he's coming out. He opens the door and heads out to the porch with his hands raised above his head.

The Lieutenant in charge has a loudspeaker. He asks Ronny if he's armed and Ronny tells him no. The cop instructs Ronny to walk down towards him slowly. The Lieutenant wants to know what happened. Ronny tells him the whole story and takes him into the house to show him the bullet hole in the window and the bullet still lodged in the living room wall.

He also shows the cop the Restraining Order the Judge issued against the hillbilly landlord. Ronny tells the cop, "If that crazy old bastard comes near this house or my family again, the only one they'll need to call is the morgue."

The cop suggests that might not be the best way to handle the situation but he'll pass on the message to the landlord. And that is how a dog bite led to the not so great Kentucky Standoff.

Smooth Operator

Ronny learned a lot about how to treat various ailments over his long racing career treating horses. As a result, he developed a cosmetic clay mask that reduced swelling and wrinkles, and created smooth skin. The only problem he encountered with the product was the smell. In order to market it successfully, it had to smell better. While in Louisiana he met a beautiful woman who happened to be an expert cosmetician. She helped Ronny solve the fragrance issue. Ronny and the woman fell in love.

The product worked extremely well and Ronny went around selling it to various salons and beauty franchises. Even one of the big cosmetic firms was interested in the product but Ronny found they only really wanted to steal his formula. The product was called Smooth Operator. He even had his lawyer trademark the name. He had labels, pamphlets, and product packaging designed and printed. Everything was going great until the lawyer's letters started to arrive.

Ronny contacted his lawyer who tells him the letters are coming from a fancy Washington law firm that works for one of the big

Hollywood studios. They've issued Ronny a cease and desist order, threatening a lawsuit if he doesn't immediately remove all Smooth Operator products from the shelves, and cease using the name in the future.

The studio had a cartoon character that went by the same name and they felt Ronny's use of the name would cause confusion and untold harm to their reputation and brand. Ronny applied for, and received, an official trademark from the United States Patent and Trademark Office so he wasn't worried. His lawyer filed an injunction stopping the Hollywood studio from proceeding. The injunction cost fifteen hundred dollars. Every month for the next five months this legal skirmish continued, and every month Ronny received a bill from his lawyer for fifteen hundred dollars.

Finally he had enough. He owed the lawyer seventy-five hundred dollars and he just couldn't afford to continue this battle indefinitely. He went to his lawyer to discuss his options. Ronny figured he had the trademark so he should be in the clear.

The lawyer explains that defending the trademark might take five years and it would surely bankrupt him even if he eventually won the case. His only option, according to his lawyer was to comply with the studio's demands and change the name. That too would be costly.

"The hell with that," says Ronny. "Give me the name of the guy in charge of the studio, I'll call him directly."

"You can't do that," says the lawyer.

"Watch me! Now give me the *putz's* name.

The lawyer gives Ronny the studio head's name and Ronny calls him. The boss's secretary answers the phone. She is aware of who he is. She connects him to her boss.

"Good afternoon Mr. Kleinberg, what can I do for you?"

"You can stop harassing and threatening me for starters."

"Mr. Kleinberg, you stop using the name Smooth Operator, and we'll stop sending you cease and desist letters."

"I don't think you understand. I have this very official looking letter from the U.S. Patent and Trademark Office with an eagle on it and everything, that says Ronny Kleinberg owns the trademark on Smooth Operator."

"What you don't understand, Mr. Kleinberg, my friend…"

Ronny interrupts. "Let's get one thing straight, I'm not your friend!"

"Be that as it may, our company is grandfathered for the name. We've been in business for fifty years; you've been in business for a year. The name is ours."

"I see from your filings you've trademarked all your other characters, why didn't you trademark Smooth Operator? It looks to me as if you didn't do it intentionally."

"It was an oversight, but…"

"But nothing. You're going to lose. If you don't stop bothering me I'll sue you for three hundred thousand dollars."

"What?"

"You heard me, three hundred thousand dollars! That's a lot of dough even for a big studio like yours. But I'm a reasonable person so here's what I'm prepared to do... I'll take thirty thousand and I'll change the name. When can I expect the check?"

"Why should I send you any money?"

"It will cost me money to change the name, refile with the trademark office, and design and print new labels, brochures, and packaging. You're creating a lot of extra work and expense. You've got till Monday noon to agree or I take this to the next step."

"The next step? What is that, a threat?"

"No, it's not a threat, it's a promise. If you don't agree to my terms, the next call I make is to Oprah. Just imagine poor little me, just an average working stiff trying to eke out a living being pushed around and bankrupted by some big bad Hollywood conglomerate. By the time I'm finished making the rounds of every afternoon talk show, there's not a mother in North America that will let her kids watch your cartoons." Ronny hangs up.

On Monday noon Ronny calls the studio head. "So do we have a deal or not?" says Ronny.

"I'm authorized to send you a check for fifteen thousand to cover your expenses."

"I don't think you understand. This is not a negotiation. Either you send me the full thirty thousand in twenty-four hours or my next calls are to Oprah and the television news networks."

"Give me five minutes Mr. Kleinberg?"

"Take six, but make it fast." Ten minutes later the studio boss is back on the line agreeing to Ronny's terms.

THE END

One phone call from Sal and the problem is solved.
Learn more in "The Fixer" - Rebel Seed Publishing

Bonus Material

Below are a few tips that will help you even the playing field.

Ten Things You Need To Know To Win At The Racetrack
The Fixer's Formula For Winning At The Racetrack

1. Never bet the Daily Double, it's a sucker's bet. It's hard enough to pick one winner let alone forcing yourself to pick two consecutive winners. (1a) Never bet on all the races on a racing card, only bet the best four or five races that give you the best chance to win.

2. Never bet first time starters. They have no track record and you never know what first time starters are going to do.

3. Never bet the trifecta. Trying to pick the first three finishers in a race in the correct order is for suckers. Forget about it.

4. Never bet on horses that haven't run in the last thirty days. Chances are there is something wrong with them.

5. Horses are generally run in what are called 'conditions' which means horses that have never won or have won only one or two races should run against other horses in the same category. Never bet on a horse that is running out of his class, for example, never bet a none winner who is running against horses that have won four or five races.

6. Look for a horse that has had consistent good results over their last ten races. If a horse consistently finished first, second, third, or fourth in their last ten races, it's a good bet its got a chance to win or at least finish in the money.

These are the kinds of horses you want to bet when betting an Exactor (must pick the horses that finish first and second in the exact order) or a Pick 3 (must pick the winners in three consecutive races before the first race begins). If you're lucky, a long shot will win one of the races, resulting in a good payday. The minimum bet is only $0.20 per horse so the investment is minimal.

7. The Pick 3 is the best type of exotic bet. Check the program for three races in a row where two of the races have short fields, meaning only five horses are running. Bet on every horse in those two races, and pick the best three horses in the remaining race. If two short fields aren't available use the other tips to eliminate the obvious losers.

8. Horse racing can be the best way to gamble because the Daily Racing Form gives you all the information you need. Learn what all the stats mean and how to use them.

9. Horse racing not only gives you all the pertinent facts and figures of a horse's past performances, you can visually check out the horses

just before race time to see if the animal looks lame or is overly excited. Stay away from sweating horses that are jumping around wasting energy before they get into the starting gate.

10. One statistic that you can look out for is the Speed Rating. The Speed Rating measures a horse's previous performances against the track record. The horse with the best Speed Rating in similar races under the same conditions will usually run first or second.

Ten More Things You Need To Know To Win At The Racetrack
How To Bet At The Track – The Fixer's Legal Formula

1. If you really want a chance to win at the track you have to learn how to read the "The Daily Racing Form" or a program that shows past performances.

2. Eliminate the bad trainers and the bad jockeys.

3. The Speed Rating for the track record is designated as 100, so eliminate any horse with a Speed Rating under 80.

4. Eliminate horses that are too active before the race. They're wasting energy.

5. Eliminate horses that lost their last race by more than 10 lengths, unless its been dropped down in class by 1/2 (eg. from a $20,000 claimer to a $10,000 claimer).

6. Eliminate horses that have not run in the last 30 days.

7. Once you're eliminated all the horses you don't want to bet on, start looking for horses whose trainer and jockey are Rated 1, 2, or 3.

8. Look for horses that consistently finish 1st, 2nd, 3rd or 4th.

9. Look for horses with Speed Ratings over 80: average the Speed Rating for horses at the same track at the same distance and pick the horse with the highest average rating.

10. Look for horses that have won the most money.

Learn more in "The Fixer" - Rebel Seed Publishing
Paperback: amzn.to/2mfvgMa • eBook: amzn.to/1ZoJCMe

www.ingramcontent.com/pod-product-compliance
Lightning Source LLC
Chambersburg PA
CBHW070051080526
44586CB00013B/1013